best man's last-minute organiser

essentials

wendy hobson

foulsham
LONDON • NEW YORK • TORONTO • SYDNEY

foulsham

The Publishing House, Bennetts Close,
Cippenham, Slough, Berks, SL1 5AP, England

ISBN 0-572-02975-6

Copyright © 2004 W. Foulsham & Co. Ltd

Cover photograph © Powerstock

A CIP record for this book is available from the British Library

Printed in Great Britain by Cox & Wyman Ltd, Reading

Contents

Introduction

I considered starting this book with the opening lines from *Four Weddings and a Funeral* but it's been done before and anyway that would be plagiarism! Still, the fact that you have bought this book – or perhaps, in desperation, someone has given it to you – means we are entering panic mode.

It could be that your best friend has been swept off his feet in a whirlwind romance and there's just three weeks before they tie the knot. However, I think the following scenario is probably more likely.

You remember that evening about 18 months ago when your best mate astonished you by announcing that his girlfriend was indeed the woman of his dreams and she had agreed to marry him? Well, you probably don't remember much of it, but the beginning must be fairly clear and the rest is probably best forgotten. Anyway, you'll have had a cracking night and probably ended up punching each other playfully on the upper arm and swearing you'd always be mates and it wouldn't change a thing. You might even – perhaps something that could now haunt your waking moments – have mumbled something fairly incoherent about how you couldn't have a better best friend in the world and what an honour it was to be asked to be his best man.

Well, however distasteful this mushy stuff may be, the fact remains that he *is* your best mate, you are still chuffed to bits to have been asked to be his best man, and you don't want to let him down.

So how did you get to three weeks from the actual day without giving it more than a fleeting thought, then brushing it aside thinking you still had plenty of time? It happens – don't worry about it. The very fact that you are reading this book indicates that there are enough last-minute best men out there to make it a commercial publishing proposition – so you are in good company.

And to flatter you even more – although quite why I should be doing that when the bride, if no one else, would be the first to say you've messed up, I'm not sure – is that you have made a very wise decision in picking up this little book. Although it may be true that you have dug yourself a nice deep hole, you have now equipped yourself with the tools not only to fill it in, but also to smooth it over and emerge sweat-free and dusted off, ready for action.

Here you have a day-by-day programme of what needs to be done, why, where, with whom and when. It is based on having about three weeks before the big day. You may have more or less time, so you can adjust the timetable to suit yourself. If you're a last-hour best man, you may congratulate yourself on being further ahead than others and use it as a checklist and reminder of the things that you *have* left until the last minute. If you're a last-second best man, just get a move on will you?

I've tried to include everything you need to know and need to do as best man. The information is based on what is traditionally expected, and for the most part that applies to a church wedding. Register office weddings are generally quicker and less formal. Nowadays, however, weddings are being held in a variety of locations and as the events become less traditional, couples are making their own rules and changing things to suit themselves. The only way you are going to find out if that's the case for you is to discuss the details with the bride and groom. You can't go far wrong if you start with the accepted practice and go on from there.

There's only one rule in this last-minute organiser: decide what needs to be done and just DO IT!

- You don't have the time for prevarication or indecision.
- You'll get nowhere if you run around in circles.
- You'll drop everything if you try to juggle too many things at once.

Take one step at a time. Make a decision, act on it, then move on to the next item on the agenda. If you do decide to postpone something until another day, don't postpone it indefinitely, write it down to be done on a specific day. Unfortunately, just reading this book won't get the job done. I'll do my best for you, but it's time for you to get moving!

P.S. In the event that you are a female last-minute best man, I'm afraid you'll have to put up with the use of the male pronoun throughout the book. The role is the same whatever your gender, so it makes no difference to your planning. The only female gender-specific comment I would make is to make sure that nothing you wear and nothing you do comes even close to upstaging the bride.

The Help-yourself Rules

There aren't really any rules because the only thing that matters is that you end up a great best man. These are just basic, common sense tips that will help you to achieve that.

K.I.S.S.
It is much more impressive to do something simply and do it really well, than to try to do something too complicated and muddle through it, so the old marketing rule is a good one: 'Keep It Simple, Stupid.'

One thing at a time
Don't stress over everything that has to be done. Plan what you are going to do, take one thing at a time and do it, then move on.

Keep it together
Especially if you are a back-of-the-envelope man, decide now that you are going to write everything in this book. That way, you won't lose anything, it will all be to hand when you want it, and you'll save time and stress searching for those vital phone numbers you jotted down on the gas bill envelope that your flatmate has now used as a shopping list. You are not going to use the book again, so use it as a workbook. Cross things out

that don't apply and customise the lists to suit yourself; write in numbers, names or things to do. Tick things off when they are done. Jot down the 'safe places' you choose for important items. Once the wedding is over, you are going to chuck out the book anyway, so get scribbling.

Remember why you are doing this

This is about being there for your best mate. It's his and his fiancée's big day and you want to help them to make it really special. You may not normally go for wearing a carnation in your buttonhole or shaking hands with strange, middle-aged ladies in hats but, just for today, that's what it takes.

Three minutes is not a long time

The thing most best men dread the most is the speech. Don't worry. Firstly, we have all sorts of tips to help you write a genuine and amusing speech. Secondly, remember that the longest best man's speech should only last about three minutes. That's about how long it takes to down a pint if you only sip it – how hard can it be? Don't worry – you can do it.

You won't lose it

The second item on the 'best man worries' list is that you'll lose the rings or drop them down some handy grating in the church floor.

Firstly, for the price of a packet of Post-it Notes, strategically placed (what did we ever do without them?), you can make sure you don't forget anything you need to take on the day. Make a decision on which pocket the rings are going in and stick to it, then you won't break into a cold sweat when you look for them in the wrong place because you'll know where they are. How simple is that?

Then, let's deal with the grating. That's all about being sensible. How many times have you watched a film where the heroine, alone in the house and perfectly well aware that there's a crazed killer on the loose, goes down into the cellar in her skimpy nightie – without turning the light on, mind you – because she's heard a noise in the night? Does she grab her mobile, lock herself in the bathroom, call the police and scream the place down to attract the neighbours like any sensible person? No, she doesn't, because doing that would ruin the plot.

For you, the opposite works. If there is a grating, the rings stay in your pocket. You are not Frodo and rings do not have a will of their own; leave them where they can't come to any harm. When you are standing safely in your own hallway about to leave for the church, that's the time to check that the rings are in the designated pocket. When you are sitting safely in the pew as the guests arrive, that's the time to double-check. When you are carrying the box of buttonholes and running past a group of choirboys along the gravel path from the church car park to the vestry – well, what do you think?

Relax and enjoy

If you know you are well prepared – and you can do that by working through this book – you can really relax on the day and the whole experience will be much more enjoyable.

You can also help everyone else to relax. A wedding is an emotional occasion, especially for the women (if you don't feel it, just trust me). It's also very stressful. All the major players have invested heavily in time, energy and emotion – not to mention a huge stack of money – and now it's time to put it all to the test. There's no second chances, no room to say, 'It'll go all right tomorrow.' Plus, those key players don't just want it to work, they want it to be stupendous!

Mix emotion, stress, intense anticipation and high expectations and you have a potential explosion! Do you wander around casually flicking your cigarette lighter? (For the literal-minded, that means, playing a 'joke' on the bride's mother by telling her you've just run over that big box by the front step marked 'The Fabulous Florist' and does it matter?) Laugh now, if you want, but the answer is 'No!' With a little thought and some well-timed words or gestures, you can be the one to defuse any tense situations. The calmer everyone is, the smoother the day will go, and the more everyone will enjoy themselves. You can help to achieve that.

Finally, just do it!

If you're a last-minute best man, you've done enough putting off. Now is the time to get on with what needs to be done. You can do it. And I happen to think you'll be a great best man.

The Countdown

No one has all the time in the world to pore over instructions on what to do – and I think we can safely presume you don't have much inclination for that anyway – so the plan is to keep everything in bite-sized chunks and do a bit each day, so you can see genuine progress – that's very encouraging and will help keep you going. That way, you can still have time for work, of course, training, the gym, origami classes – whatever you do with your spare time. All you need to do is set aside a couple of hours each day for the designated task.

The early Countdown Days are slightly fuller than some of the later ones, the idea being that if you get ahead you will feel much more relaxed as you get nearer to the wedding day. The more relaxed you are, the more you will enjoy it. It also allows for some time to catch up with anything you haven't managed to do on the 'due' dates.

If you want to compensate for your busy evenings, you can simply do two things on the previous day and get ahead, or squeeze the task into your lunch-hour. Some jobs can easily be combined, some you may want to spend more time on – like writing your speech. You may need to change the jobs around a bit, depending on your own commitments and the day of the week. That's all possible within the plan.

Inevitably there will be a bit of overlap in the information, but you should use that to familiarise yourself with the whole event, which will actually help you enjoy it more because you will feel more comfortable about what is going to happen. Don't pass up the opportunity to use it to double-check that everything has been done, and done well. The only rule here is that you don't use the fact that you can't do something on a specific Countdown Day as an excuse not to do it at all.

If you don't want to work in sound-bites but prefer to set aside a complete day at the weekend to accomplish everything listed for the week, that will work just as well; although be warned that it doesn't allow any room for manoeuvre should anything go wrong. We don't have to worry about that however, because from now on it's all going to be plain sailing.

The countdown

Countdown Day 21 What Does a Best Man Actually Do?
Countdown Day 20 Where, When and Who?
Countdown Day 19 Sort Out Your Diary
Countdown Day 18 Organise the Stag Night
Countdown Day 17 What Are You Going to Wear?
Countdown Day 16 How to Get There – and How to Get Back
Countdown Day 15 The Rehearsal of the Ceremony
Countdown Day 14 Are the Ushers Up To Speed?
Countdown Day 13 Write Your Speech
Countdown Day 12 Get Clued Up about the Reception

Countdown Day 21

What Does a Best Man Actually Do?

Today's task
- Find out what being a best man is all about and what is likely to be expected of you.

Why do I need to do that?
- We've already said that weddings cost a lot of time, energy, stress and money. The bride, especially, is likely to have very high expectations, and that will include what she expects you to do. If you know what you are doing, you can relax and enjoy yourself.

What to do
- Read this chapter. Cross out anything that doesn't apply in your case, make notes on things you need to find out about or special things to remember.

What not to do
- Skip this chapter! You don't want any surprises.

The best man's role

The best man is supposed to be the groom's right-hand man during the run-up to the wedding and on the wedding day itself. Originally, he would have been the chief negotiator with the bride's father for the 'price' of the bride's hand, but if you think that mentioning that is likely to raise a laugh with the bride in your speech at the reception, you can forget it now!

In this section, we'll run through the basic outline of what the day has in store and what you are expected to do. The idea is to get the general pattern of the day. We'll go through what's expected in more detail later on so don't worry too much about specifics today. If you do have any particular worries, though, jot them down and make sure they are answered when you get to the main sections.

Qualities of a best man

Every virtue you possess, of course!

Well organised
Well, you have the book, don't you?

Well informed
Ditto.

Level-headed
If you don't have common sense, stick to the rules in the book.

Punctual

Either you are naturally punctual or you are not. If you are, there's no problem. If you are not – and under the circumstances this seems more likely – decide now that you are going to be punctual for the next three weeks. How? It just takes a little advance planning – who knows, you might even get a taste for it.

- Sort out your diary so that you know where you are meant to be and when.
- Spend a few minutes working out how you are going to get there and how long it will take.
- Add 10 per cent.
- Set off in good time.
- Mend your alarm clock.

Sober

There are only two days when this matters. You should take responsibility for getting the groom safely home after the stag night, not leave him chained to the lamp-post in the high street. If you think you are going to mess up, go for Plan B and ask someone else to pick you up/check you are still breathing/check the groom is where he should be at a designated time.

On the wedding day, you may well feel the need for a bit of Dutch courage, but keep it to just one – at least before you do your speech.

Thoughtful
Look out for the groom, of course, but try to keep an eye out on the wedding day for anyone who needs a helping hand: for instance, the elderly aunt who would just love a turn around the dance floor; the kids who are bored rigid and will play up if they don't find something to eat soon; the 13-year-old bridesmaid who's tripped up on her dress and feels a complete idiot but could be rescued by a fit guy asking her to dance. You should recognise plenty of potential there for making yourself the man of the moment.

Before the wedding
You've left it a bit late for some of this, so I assume that the bride and groom have already taken care of most of this bit. Some grooms expect the best man to help him choose the ushers, buy his clothes and book the cars for the bride to the church and the bride and groom to the reception. If he hasn't done that by now, you're in trouble, so just tactfully check that it's all in hand.

In the unlikely event that it has not been organised, work out what is needed and get on the phone straight away to see what bookings you can get with local wedding car hire companies. With no time to spare, it'll be a time to compromise. You may not be able to get the white Rolls-Royce she wanted, so see what you can get. As long as it has a bit of style, you'll be okay.

The best man and the ushers hand out the order-of-service

sheets at the church and show guests to their seats, so you may have to collect the necessary items before the wedding.

The stag night

It's your job to organise the stag party and to see the groom home safely at the end of it. The first bit is easy. The second may require some contingency planning, but that's all dealt with on Countdown Days 18 and 7.

On the wedding day morning

It's crunch time. You must get the groom to the ceremony venue on time, sober, smart, with all the documents, money, rings and anything else he needs. He'll also need his going-away kit and honeymoon luggage.

You'll liaise with the ushers to make sure the wedding party have their buttonholes and corsages (fancy buttonholes for the ladies), ensure guests can park their cars and are then shown to their seats with an order-of-service sheet, if there is one. You'll take charge of the rings and you won't lose them. You'll also make sure the groom has paid all the church fees and look after the money, if necessary.

At the ceremony

Basically, you stick with the groom. You sit at the front with him, then stand when the music starts to announce the arrival of the bride. You remain just behind and to the right of the groom until you are told to sit down. You hand over the rings when prompted by whoever is officiating.

Once the ceremony itself is over, you escort the chief bridesmaid to where the register is signed, and you may be asked to sign the register as a witness, then escort her from the church or ceremony venue. You'll help organise the guests for the photographs and off to the reception venue. You may drive the bridesmaids, or just go with the wedding party, in which case you'll need to make sure the chief usher knows he has to be the last to leave and make sure everyone is safely on their way to the reception and nothing – and no one – has been left behind. The other option is that you leave last.

At the reception

There are various levels of formality at a reception and that will set the tone for how the event is organised.

At a formal reception, you will be among the first to arrive and will join the bride and groom and both sets of parents to welcome the guests. You may have to act as master of ceremonies and introduce the guests as they arrive. On less formal occasions, you may be asked to offer drinks, take charge of coats or generally make sure guests know where to go when they arrive. At the wedding breakfast – as the first meal the couple enjoy together is called – you may be asked to help people to find their seats, or just to encourage the ushers to do so. You'll sit with the wedding party.

When it is time for the speeches, you may have to act as master of ceremonies again and introduce the speakers. You respond to the toast to the bridesmaids and talk a bit about the groom, reading out any telemessages and announcing the cutting of the cake. Then there's the dancing or entertainment and you can relax!

Finally, it's up to you to decorate the couple's going-away car and make sure it is loaded with their luggage, and check that they have all the honeymoon documents. You can also lend a hand in making sure all the guests leave safely and in clearing up, including taking care of the groom's wedding suit. Usually, the bride's parents take care of the wedding presents, but occasionally that falls to the best man.

After the wedding

After it's all over, you can breathe a great sigh of relief! You usually take charge of returning any hired wedding suits. You probably need to write a thank-you letter for any gift you have received from the bride and groom, but that's about it. Apart from congratulating yourself on a job well done, of course.

Today's top tip: keep it cool

With the notable exception of the prospect of your speech, you may be fairly phlegmatic about this whole thing, which is a good way to be. However, the people most closely involved will be taking it very seriously. Quite apart from the fact that two people are about to make a major commitment, the organisation of the wedding has been planned like a military operation for months. The bride wants it to be the happiest and most splendid day of her life. The groom could well be in a complete flat spin coping with everything he has to do, plus the rising stress levels of surrounding females. The mums have worried about everything from whether the prospective partner is good enough for their baby to not wanting to look like the caricature 'mother-of-the-bride'. Battling for the top of the bride's dad's list are likely to be losing his little girl and how is he going to pay for all this. Feelings are running high.

One job that you can take on as best man is to help keep everything on an even keel and there are two very simple ways in which you can help.

The first is to give a hand to solve practical problems. If you find out that the groom is supposed to be picking up the order-of-service sheets from the printers at the same time as he is giving an important presentation at the office, step in and offer to pick them up for him. Don't keep it to yourself. If anyone – usually the bride or her mum – is worried, tell them you have it all in hand and you'll drop off the package at such-and-such a time. Then do it.

The second is to be alert to rising panic! It's like when the sauce in the pan is just about to boil over but you turn off the heat just in time to avoid a disgusting mess on the cooker. It doesn't matter in the slightest whether you understand what all the fuss is about, just remain calm, at least pretend you are understanding, and offer a simple, practical solution to whatever the problem may be. It might be as simple as making a cup of tea for the bride's mum and making her sit down for five minutes – especially if you fancied a brew yourself anyway! Put yourself about and become known as that 'nice young man' and you'll be remembered for ever!

Countdown Day 20
Where, When and Who?

Today's task
- Check and write down all the details of the wedding and the people involved.

Why do I need to do that?
- You need to be in the right place at the right time. It will impress everyone if you know who they are – but you risk offending them if you get important people mixed up.

What to do
- Check your invitation, talk to the groom and the bride and find out exactly what is happening when, who with and what they expect of you.

What not to do
- Don't guess or miss anything out because you think you'll remember – that'll be the one thing that slips your mind.

How do I get the information?

Start with your invitation. That will contain the crucial details. Fill that into your list first.

Then arrange to get together with the groom over a quiet pint or call him at a convenient time when neither of you will be interrupted. Don't do it in a busy pub or at the office. You are bound to be distracted or interrupted and you'll miss out something vital. Make it a friendly and relaxing time.

Don't alarm the poor chap by giving him the impression that you have left everything to the last minute. Reassure him and show how super-efficient you are by telling them that you have everything in hand and you are just going through your final countdown and want one last check that everything is in order. Use the checklist on pages 30–35 as your prompt sheet. Ask him for the names and details of the wedding party – that's the parents, bridesmaids and ushers. Check whether he knows about the rehearsal or whether there are any pre-wedding get-togethers you are expected to attend.

You may find that he runs out of information at a crucial point. That's when you need to get hold of the bride so you can fill in everything else. The advantage of filling in as much as you can before you speak to the bride is that she's likely to be disconcerted if she sees too many blank spaces. Give her a call to chat it through, or pop round to see her with your planner. It's even more important that you don't spook her so near to the wedding day by letting her think you're doing everything at the last minute. Tell her you are missing some details – something not too important like the ushers' telephone numbers, or whether her dad expects to be invited to the stag night – and then say that while you've got her on the phone, perhaps you could run through everything just to make sure.

Alternatively, of course, you might like to invite the pair of them round to supper and do it all in one go.

The importance of detail

Since it is a sad fact that quite a few parents are likely to be separated or divorced, make sure you are quite clear if this is the case, and that you understand how it will be handled. Many couples are quite relaxed about the whole thing; others not so. You need to know if there are any issues to be avoided. For example, at some weddings, they split the top table so that divorced parents don't have to sit together; you need to know this in advance. Try to find out a little about the groom's mother, if you don't already know her, as you are likely to be sitting next to her at the reception. This way you'll have some conversational gambits to help break the ice.

Be sure to ask if anyone needs any special attention, such as a VIP guest or an elderly relative in a wheelchair. Find out if there are any family issues to deal with: never talk to Uncle Albert in front of Auntie Maureen, for example!

Always clarify locations, where necessary, and clarify times exactly. If the bride is talking about the time the ceremony starts and you think she's talking about the time to arrive at the church, I don't need to tell you that's bad news.

Don't miss out something because you think you won't need it. If you are right and you don't need it, you'll only have wasted a few minutes. If it is the one thing you wish you'd jotted down for a potential emergency, you'll kick yourself.

Where to keep the information

I'm going to assume that you are going to use this little book to record everything, from names and numbers to don't-forget-lists and appointments. That way there will be no confusion; you can't lose slips of paper or write some things in the book and others somewhere else – a sure-fire recipe for disaster. You may prefer to use your ordinary diary, a special notebook for the purpose, or whatever. The crucial thing is that everything is in one sensible place. Keep it with you at all times, then you won't be tempted back to the back-of-the-receipt notes that are always so determined to go astray.

Get ahead – book the stag night

While you are checking dates, fix the date for the stag night with the groom for the week before the wedding, or whatever is convenient. You can then get down to the organisation in a few days' time.

Today's top tip: block capitals
There's a reason that most forms you have to fill in have 'Please write clearly in block capitals in blue or black ink' written at the top. Don't just scribble down names or numbers in your worst end-of-the-day scrawl. Write clearly so you have no problem reading what you have written when you need it and be especially carefully with telephone numbers and e-mail addresses.

The crucial information

Rehearsal

Date . . . .
Time . . . .
Venue . . . .

Stag night

Date . . . .
Time . . . .
Venue . . . .

Pre-wedding parties or events

Event . . . .
Date . . . .
Time . . . .
Venue . . . .

Event ....

Date ....

Time ....

Venue ....

The wedding day
Date ....

The ceremony
Venue ....

Address ....

....

Telephone ....

Minister or registrar's name ....

Arrival time at the church ....

Time of ceremony ....

The reception
Venue ....

Address ....

....

Telephone ....

Contact name ....

Arrival time at the reception ....

Time couple are leaving the reception ....

Time reception finishes ....

The wedding party

In case you haven't come across the term yet, the 'wedding party' means all the principle people involved in the wedding. Simply fill in all the details, which the groom or bride will be able to supply.

The groom will probably have chosen the ushers already but, if not, you can give him a hand in making a short list and asking them if they are willing to take on the role. There is usually about one usher to every 50 or so guests – with one person designated 'chief usher' – and the groom's and bride's brothers and best friends are usually asked to help. With the more relaxed modern etiquette, there's no reason why they shouldn't be female friends as well.

Bride . . . .
Address . . . .
Telephone . . . .
Mobile . . . .
E-mail . . . .

Groom . . . .
Address . . . .
Telephone . . . .
Mobile . . . .
E-mail . . . .

Bride's parents . . . .
Address . . . .
Telephone . . . .
Mobile . . . .
E-mail . . . .
Notes . . . .

Groom's parents . . . .
Address . . . .
Telephone . . . .
Mobile . . . .
E-mail . . . .
Notes . . . .

Chief bridesmaid . . . .
Address . . . .
Telephone . . . .
Mobile . . . .
E-mail . . . .

Other bridesmaids . . . .
. . . .
. . . .
. . . .
. . . .
. . . .

Chief usher . . . .
Address . . . .
Telephone . . . .
Mobile . . . .
E-mail . . . .

Usher 1 . . . .
Address . . . .
Telephone . . . .
Mobile . . . .
E-mail . . . .

Usher 2 . . . .
Address . . . .
Telephone . . . .
Mobile . . . .
E-mail . . . .

Usher 3 . . . .
Address . . . .
Telephone . . . .
Mobile . . . .
E-mail . . . .

Usher 4 . . . .
Address . . . .
Telephone . . . .
Mobile . . . .
E-mail . . . .

Special guests

. . . .
. . . .
. . . .
. . . .
. . . .
. . . .
. . . .
. . . .
. . . .

Today's top tip: be mobile
Save the land-line and mobile numbers of all the wedding party into your handset now so you have them if and when you need them.

Countdown Day 19
Sort Out Your Diary

Today's task
- Make sure all the times, dates and places-to-be are written clearly in one place. Cancel anything that gets in the way of your wedding plans and make any appointments necessary.

Why do I need to do that?
- Three weeks is not long to get everything done and you can only be in one place at a time. You need to be organised and focused.

What to do
- Write down every wedding-related date that is already fixed, and all your existing appointments and commitments that you can't cancel. Cancel everything else. Then start to fill in the remaining appointments.

What not to do
- Don't use two diaries – keep everything for the next few weeks in one place – and don't miss anything out.

Where to keep the diary

As I said yesterday, I'm assuming that all your information is going to be kept in this book so there's less chance of confusion or, in this case, missed appointments. If you are using your own diary for everything, that's fine. Whichever it is, keep it clearly written, up-to-date – and keep it with you.

I've worked the diary below on the basis that the wedding is on a Saturday, but change it round if the wedding is on a different day. It's then a step-by-step process. As long as you are methodical, you can't go wrong.

Record the wedding events

First, write down in the diary section on pages 40–42 the wedding date and time.

Then add the dates of all the wedding-related events that have already been organised, such as:

- The stag night.
- The rehearsal.

Depending on how last-minute you have left everything, other events may already have been organised, or you will need to write them in your diary once they are fixed, such as:

- Meeting the ushers.
- Meeting the bridesmaids.
- Meeting the parents.

Check and double-check to make sure nothing is forgotten.

Sort out your regular commitments

Now go through your own diary – whether it's on paper or in your head – and write down all your existing commitments, including work and all the boring but essential things you have to do on a regular basis.

If you get to something that is not essential but might put you under pressure, cancel it immediately before you move on. Make the telephone call or send the e-mail straight away – don't think you'll do it later. It might be that you meet your mates in the pub on a Thursday after work, or you give someone a lift to the gym. Just call to let them know you won't make it for these few weeks, or whatever. If you find you are ahead of the game come the day, you can always change your mind and go, but you'll have taken the pressure off yourself by doing it this way round.

What else do you need to do?

Now you need to think about what else needs to be done before the wedding. Look at the list below and see what you need to do. Glance forward to the tasks for specific Countdown Days, make the appointments and write them down. There are bound to be other things that apply specifically to your circumstances, so write them down, too.

- Buy your suit or collect from the hire centre (Countdown Day 17).
- Book a dancing lesson (Countdown Day 11).

- Go on a shopping trip for the present and anything else you need (Countdown Day 9).
- Book an appointment for a haircut (Countdown Day 6) or any other pampering you fancy (within reason).
- Have the car serviced and valeted (Countdown Day 2).
- Drive the route (Countdown Day 3).

Keep your diary up-to-date

As other things are organised, make sure you refer back to your diary to fill them in. That way you won't double-book anything.

As an added bonus, the bride will also find it hugely reassuring that if she rings to book you for something, you check with your diary and write it down as you are talking! Start now in getting yourself known as Mr Reliable!

Your wedding countdown diary

Day	Date	Event	Location	Action
Sunday				
Monday				
Tuesday				
Wednesday				
Thursday				
Friday				
Saturday				

Your wedding countdown diary

Day	Date	Event	Location	Action
Sunday				
Monday				
Tuesday				
Wednesday				
Thursday				
Friday				
Saturday				

Your wedding countdown diary

Day	Date	Event	Location	Action
Sunday				
Monday				
Tuesday				
Wednesday				
Thursday				
Friday				
Saturday				

Today's top tip: be realistic
Be realistic about what you can and cannot achieve in this short space of time and you won't leave anything to chance. If you have two appointments in one evening, for example, ask yourself whether you have allowed enough travel time to get from one to the other. What is the likelihood of getting caught by the boss at work or a meeting running over so you'll be late if you cut your timing too fine? Apply the same priority rules to this organisation as you do at work. Do the most important things first, then fit the rest in around them.

Countdown Day 18
Organise the Stag Night

Today's task
- Organise the stag night for a week before the wedding.

Why do I have to do that?
- You don't need an answer to that one!

What to do
- Confirm the date, time and arrangements with the groom, and then check with everyone he would like to attend.

What not to do
- Forget that you have to get all the guests – especially the groom – home safely.

When should it be?
Traditionally the stag night is the groom's last night of freedom before he is married. In the past it was actually held on the night before the wedding. Fortunately, that's now changed and it is

usually held on the Saturday before the wedding. I have already suggested on Countdown Day 20 that you fix the date with the groom while you are checking on all the other wedding events, so you should have the date already. If not, check to see what is convenient for the groom and make a decision. Write it down in your diary and on the checklist on page 50.

Who comes to the stag night?

Usually an all-male affair – although this is changing – and those who attend are all the groom's closest friends, including his brothers if he has any. This will include all the ushers, of course.

Traditionally, the groom's father and future father-in-law are invited, although if they do come it is accepted practice for them to leave half way through the evening so they don't spoil your fun. It really depends on whether they are likely to muck in and enjoy the evening or cast a shadow over the revelry by hating every minute of it! It's up to the groom whether you go along with this idea and invite them, but do make sure no one is left out if the groom would like them to be included.

Chat it through with the groom and make a guest list in the checklist on pages 51–2, and write down all the contact phone numbers and e-mail addresses.

Where should we go?

Decide with the groom what sort of evening you would like. The most popular arrangement is a meal followed by a pub – or pubs – or perhaps a club. It's all a matter of where you'll most enjoy yourselves.

You may already know the perfect place. If not, think about places you do know and see if they might fit the bill. It's probably better to go somewhere where you know – or are reliably informed – you'll have a good time. Check opening and closing times, if necessary, and make your choice – or choices.

Book any tables or special rooms, if necessary. If you are not sure of the numbers of people, make your best guess and make the booking, then confirm it when everyone has let you know whether or not they will be able to come.

Agree a convenient meeting point to start with. Especially if people are coming any distance, it's nice to meet in a pub so people can relax while they are waiting for everyone to arrive. Make sure everyone knows the format for the evening and where you will be going. Make arrangements to pick up the groom – and don't be late.

Who pays?

The only important thing here is that everyone knows what is expected. The groom often pays for the meal or the first round, then everyone pays for themselves. If that's the case, a kitty is generally the fairest and easiest option. Think about what you are likely to spend during the evening and decide on a contribution from each guest. Have a separate wallet or safe pocket to keep the money in and look after the kitty yourself. If you know you are lousy at keeping tabs on the money, delegate it to someone you know will do a better job.

The transport

The guests will be expected to get themselves to the initial meeting point. After that, you will all stay together and, if you are in town, probably walk between venues. It wastes a lot of the evening if you go to places that are too far apart.

This is so obvious it shouldn't need saying, but sadly statistics prove that people do still drink and drive. You can choose a designated driver for the evening, but it is by far the best bet to use taxis or arrange to be picked up by someone who is not enjoying the celebrations with you.

For getting home, public transport won't even be an option for most people, but if you have a good night bus service, that's another possibility.

For the majority of you, either pre-book your taxis or, for more flexibility, save the numbers of at least two taxi firms into your mobile before you set out. If you regularly use one firm, it can't hurt to give them a ring early in the evening to find out the waiting time and let them know you'll be calling back later.

It's your responsibility to get the groom home safely, so don't leave him stranded anywhere or lose him during the course of the evening. It won't be worth the frosty reception you'll get from the bride for the next few months!

Party all night

It's worth giving a thought to where everyone is going to spend the night. If one of you can offer your floor for everyone to crash on, it makes getting everyone home safely much cheaper and easier. Alternatively, you might need to book hotel rooms for anyone travelling a distance. Just check this out when you are making your list of who is coming.

Surprise! Surprise!

You can buy books of games and surprises – blow-up sheep and that kind of thing – if you want to organise activities for the evening. Or look on the internet if you need inspiration.

If you want to inflict any other surprises on the groom during the course of the evening, the adverts in the men's mags are obviously the place to go. Pre-pay or have the money ready, and make sure you are in the right place at the right time.

What about the ladies?

Some couples are now deciding to organise their stag and hen nights on the same night and either start out together or meet up later in the evening. Your friend will have his own ideas on whether or not he likes the idea, and will probably be the point of liaison with the bride's arrangements. If not, it will be up to you and the chief bridesmaid.

Speeches? Already?

Again, this is very much up to you and the groom and will depend on the format for the evening. Some best men like to write an amusing and informal speech for the occasion and – company allowing – generally use it as an excuse to embarrass the groom as much as possible with anecdotes of previous exploits of one kind or another. It also gives you all a chance to wish him all the best and toast his future happiness.

If you are really not into speech-making, do make sure you give a toast to the groom and wish him all the best, and do it fairly early on in the evening so you don't forget and you are all still coherent.

Special stag nights and weekends

This is unlikely to apply to you since you are making last-minute plans, but it may be of interest. Some grooms now decide to spend a bit more cash for a really exciting stag night or weekend. You can do anything from a night in Paris to bungee jumping, special stag weekends at hotels or adventure sports centres – the choice is pretty much endless.

You will find plenty of advertisements in bridal magazines, men's magazines and on the web to give you ideas or to book the whole package. The following websites might be useful:

www.stagparty.co.uk
www.stagweekends.com
www.stagnights.com
www.lastnightoffreedom.com
www.stags.org
www.thestagandhencompany.co.uk
www.designadventure.com

Since they tend to be fairly expensive weekends, make sure everyone understands how much they will be expected to pay out and exactly what it covers, so they can plan their budget accordingly. Don't try to force someone into coming along if it's clear that they can't afford it.

The details

Date . . . .

Meet at . . . .

Meeting time . . . .

Taxi firm . . . . Telephone . . . .

Taxi firm . . . . Telephone . . . .

The meal

Restaurant . . . .

Address . . . .

Telephone . . . .

Table booked for . . . . people Time booked . . . .

Who's coming?

Name . . . .
Telephone . . . . Mobile . . . .
E-mail . . . .

Name . . . .
Telephone . . . . Mobile . . . .
E-mail . . . .

Name . . . .
Telephone . . . . Mobile . . . .
E-mail . . . .

Name . . . .
Telephone . . . . Mobile . . . .
E-mail . . . .

Name . . . .
Telephone . . . . Mobile . . . .
E-mail . . . .

Name . . . .
Telephone . . . . Mobile . . . .
E-mail . . . .

Name . . . .
Telephone . . . . Mobile . . . .
E-mail . . . .

Name . . . .
Telephone . . . . Mobile . . . .
E-mail . . . .

Today's top tip: 'How much?!'
It doesn't matter how you organise who pays for what as long as everyone knows what is expected. Don't get into a situation where the guests think the groom is footing the bill and he thinks everyone is chipping in. If you think it is embarrassing to broach the subject, it will be much worse if you don't, and it could cause some ill-feeling, which is the last thing you want. Talk to the groom first to see if he is going to pay for any aspect of the evening, then simply tell the guests the financial arrangements at the same time as all the other details. 'We are meeting at the station on Saturday 4 April at 7 pm to go to Dmitri's for a meal, then on to one or two clubs nearby. Tom will be paying for the meal, but we'll have a kitty for the drinks and club entrance fees. We'll all go back to my flat afterwards so we can share the taxi fare.'

Countdown Day 17

What Are You Going to Wear?

Today's task
- Sort out all the details of what you are going to wear, including all your accessories.

Why do I have to do that?
- You can't just throw on your work suit at the last minute and expect to retain the friendship of your mate – let alone his wife.

What to do
- Find out the dress code and what is expected, list what you need and buy what you don't have.

What not to do
- Leave it to the last minute and then find the shops aren't open late the night you planned to buy your suit.

Dress styles

The bride and groom will set the style of the wedding and you will follow the same level of formality, so the first thing to do is find out what style they have chosen.

Top hat and tails

If it is a formal wedding before 3 pm you may be expected to wear a morning suit with a top hat and gloves. You don't actually have to wear the hat and gloves, just hold them in your left hand. If it is that kind of wedding, there's no way this will happen just a few short weeks before the wedding, so I won't go into too much detail here. If you don't have your own morning suit, you will go – or will have gone – with the groom to organise fittings for a hired suit. You'll then have to make arrangements to collect it in good time and return both your suit and the groom's after the wedding. Traditionally, the groom's family pays for the suit, although you will be expected to provide your shirt, socks, tie, shoes and accessories at your own expense.

Black tie

Another option for a formal wedding, especially if there is an evening reception or a ball, is that you will be expected to wear a dinner jacket. Again, you should know this by now if it's that kind of wedding. You are most likely to have to provide your own suit and accessories at your own expense. You may have your own suit, in which case, just check that it's okay and get it to the cleaners. If not, get down to a hire shop straight away. If you don't have a local Moss Bros., look in *Yellow Pages*.

Lounge suit

Far more likely, in your case, is that you will be expected to wear a smart lounge suit, in which case you will buy your own outfit. Obviously, if you can choose something that will be a useful and stylish addition to your wardrobe anyway, it makes a lot more sense, so perhaps you could use this as the excuse to buy that Armani suit you've had your eye on!

Before you make your choice, consider the season, the location and what everyone else is wearing. You want to feel stylish and comfortable yourself – but you don't want to stick out like a sore thumb. First, ask the groom about what he is wearing, as that will set the style and tone for your outfit. Most grooms tend to go for a fairly classic dark suit, in which case you can follow suit (sorry, I couldn't resist it!). On the other hand, especially if it's a summer wedding or in a less formal location, he might have decided to go for a lighter suit, or even a white suit, in which case you'd look a bit odd in the photos in your subdued black or navy. Ask if he has any preferences on what you wear. The chances are that he won't have given it much thought, but his future wife will have prompted him to make sure she gets what she wants.

Make it a stylish match

Sparing a thought for the effect in the photographs is not a bad way to focus your mind on style. It may not matter to you, but it will matter to the bride and groom as the photos are their memento of a huge day in their lives. A harmonious effect on camera is an indication that you've complemented the occasion perfectly from a style point of view. If nothing else, that's worth brownie points with the bride.

More points can be collected if you give the bride a ring to check what level of formality she expects and whether she has any colour schemes she would like you to follow. She might ask that the colour of your tie or waistcoat complements that of the bridesmaids' dresses or the flowers, for example. You might find that bizarre, but that's how these things are organised and a huge amount of thought, decision-making and planning goes into that kind of co-ordination, so you owe it to your mates to go with it. Whatever you do, don't think it won't matter if you wear your Spiderman tie to brighten up the occasion. The bride's sense of humour is very unlikely to stretch that far if everyone else has gone along with her tasteful colour scheme.

Shopping

If you actually enjoy shopping, of course, you'll want to make the most of it and you won't need any advice from me!

If you hate shopping, the way to make it as painless as

possible is to know what you want to buy and who is most likely to stock it before you set out. Most major retailers now have websites, so take a virtual tour in your lunch-hour and narrow down your options. You can then head straight for the stores where – all being well – your ideal outfit will be waiting for you.

Early-morning or late-night shopping is usually much less crowded and more civilised than shopping at weekends, and that also makes it a much less fraught experience. You'll also find that if the stores are less busy, the assistants will be more able to help you in your choice and will be happy to do so. It's a good sale for them, so they'll want to close it down and not send you next door to bolster the opposition's profits.

Especially since you are short of time, do make sure you try things on in the shops. If you leave it until you get home, you may run out of time to go back and change them. It's a huge generalisation, but women tend to be quite happy to keep trying things on until they find the right outfit, while men tend to find that a pain in the neck. As long as you are a genuine shopper, you can try on as many suits as you like in order to find the right one.

Some people like shopping alone, others prefer to go with a friend. If you like to have a second opinion, go with a friend who will be helpful – perhaps a girlfriend – not someone who will demonstrate he is bored to death after 10 minutes and can't wait to get down the pub. The groom is a good shopping companion as he has a vested interest in making sure you are kitted out in the right things, he'll know what he is wearing and can help you find something suitable.

What-you-need checklist

Personalise this checklist so you can make sure you have everything you need, and tick off each item when it is safely in your possession and ready for the big day.

Item	Colour	Style	Ready
Suit			
Waistcoat			
Shirt			
Cufflinks			
Tie			
Underwear			
Socks			
Shoes			
Belt			
Handkerchief			
Umbrella			
Spare handkerchiefs			

The extras

I've added an umbrella to the list, as this is a useful thing to put in the car just in case it rains on the day. You can help people get from their cars to the ceremony venue, or on to the reception without ruining their best outfits. It's just another really easy way to be thoughtful. Traditionally, it's a black umbrella, especially for a formal occasion, but most people would prefer any colour as long as it keeps off the rain.

The spare handkerchiefs – or a packet of tissues, but although that's more practical, it seems a little less gallant – are so you can offer one to any of the ladies who forget to pack a tissue and get emotional. It happens!

Dress rehearsal

It's not a bad idea to have a dress rehearsal with the groom once you have everything sorted out so you can double-check that neither of you has forgotten anything, especially the finer details such as cufflinks. Mark a date in your diary over the next few days. You can also double-check that your trousers are not too long as it will give you time to have them shortened properly before the big day.

Today's top tip: don't be labelled

Remember to remove all the tags and labels from your clothes, or the dry-cleaning tags if you have had a suit cleaned. Shoes usually have labels on the soles, so take them off, too. If you have brand-new shoes, make sure you wear them outside before the wedding day to be sure they are comfortable. Leather soles, especially, will be slippery if you don't allow the surface to roughen slightly by wearing them a couple of times.

How to Get There – and How to Get Back

Today's task
- Make all the transport and travel arrangements for the day.

Why do I have to do that?
- One of your main responsibilities is to get the groom to the church on time. You also transport guests to the reception.

What to do
- Check the car, the route and the road conditions.

What not to do
- Underestimate the time it will take to get to the ceremony.

What's your job?

Your job is to get the groom to the ceremony on time, assist with transport – often of the bridesmaids – to the reception, and make sure the bride and groom have their transport and luggage sorted for when they leave the reception to go on their honeymoon.

Where do you start ... and where do you finish?

You already know the locations of the ceremony and the reception and you know the dates and the times.

You also know where the groom lives, so the only thing left to check now is that he is going to be there on the night before the wedding. Is that a convenient place to stay so you don't have any problems getting to the ceremony? Will you be staying there the night before so you are both in the same place? Will it be easier for him to stay with you? Will it be easier to book a hotel room for the night, perhaps even in the ceremony venue if the whole event is being held in a hotel? It's much the best idea for both of you – and all your kit, of course – to be in the same place the night before so that you eliminate any potential problems in picking him up.

Make your decision by chatting with the groom and stick with it. All your arrangements work from there.

The route

Once you know where you are going from and to, you need to decide on the route you are going to take. If you know the area, that's not a problem. If you don't, take a look at www.multimap.com or get hold of a local *A–Z* and work out a logical route. Copy or print out a few copies of the map.

Chat to the groom, the bride, her dad or someone else who knows the area, to make sure it's the best route. There may be something you don't know about the traffic conditions, a recent change to a one-way system, a turning that's easy to miss or a good landmark on the route. Find out as much as you can. Ask, as well, if there are any road works in the area that could hold you up, and if there are any special events they know about for that day. If the annual carnival is held on the wedding day, you'll want to know about it!

I've allocated time in your countdown for a trial run of the route, but it's not a bad idea to drive over the routes at this stage as well, especially if you are not familiar with the area. That will also help you with working out your timing.

Parking

If you are going to a hotel with its own generous car park, you've got no worries, but if you are going to a church, the parking arrangements are unlikely to be as straightforward. You need to know what to expect. If the parking is limited you may be able to park at the venue, as you'll arrive first, but others may not be so lucky. Will you be able to park on the road outside? Will there be other weddings at a similar time with guests competing for space? Call the ceremony venue, if you can, or ask the bride or groom. Plot that into your planning.

It is very unlikely that you will have to pay for parking, but some halls do use public facilities. If that's the case, check the change you'll need to have on you and put it in the car in good time.

To the reception

If the ceremony and reception are at the same place, then you don't have anything to worry about here. If they are in different locations, you will be responsible for getting yourself to the reception and often, but not always, driving the bridesmaids there, too, or perhaps another member of the wedding party. Check this out so you don't go without anyone!

You therefore need to check your route from the ceremony to the reception, and the parking arrangements there, too. You are likely to be in a convoy with the bride and groom and the parents, but it's a bad idea to rely on that. Following another car is fine in theory, but it's not easy, especially in traffic. You only need the traffic lights to change to red and you'll be left stranded watching the wedding car disappearing into the distance. If you've got three bickering bridesmaids in the back seat and you don't know where to take them, you are going to wish you'd got your map with you. You might also wish you'd stayed lost when you turn up late at the reception!

The timing

You need to arrive at the ceremony venue about half an hour before the service is due to start, so obviously you have to work out exactly how long the journey will take to get there from wherever you are staying the night before. Don't forget to allow time for parking, if necessary.

Your timing will be calculated from when you actually leave the house, but make sure you allow time for packing the car, double-checking your list to make sure you have everything you need and checking through everything with the groom. See how long you think all that will take and add another 10 minutes.

Be pessimistic rather than realistic – and never be optimistic! Then the worst case scenario is that you have to sit in the car park for 20 minutes.

Timing from the ceremony to the reception is obviously less crucial, as everyone will be doing the same route, but do make sure you know when you are all expected at the reception so you can keep an eye on how long the photographs are taking and can keep things moving so the schedule doesn't go awry. The main wedding party are likely to be pretty distracted so they will appreciate your help.

The car

You will probably be using your own car. Check over the basics yourself – oil, water, tyres, screen wash, etc. – or book it in for a service, if necessary, and write the date in your diary. You don't want it to let you down. You'll need to make sure it is cleaned, polished and filled up with petrol, I've allowed you time for that later on (Countdown Day 2), and put car shampoo and polish on your shopping list (Countdown Day 9).

If your car is notoriously unreliable, it's not likely to change its character between now and the wedding, and it is likely to let you down when you most need it. If you cannot borrow a car from a friend, or use the groom's car, you will need to hire a car for the day or use a taxi, although this is not very flexible or stylish, so is really a last resort.

Ring round some hire firms and choose the best package you can find. Make sure you pick it up the day before and return it the day after rather than risking running out of time at either end of the day.

The decorations

If you are driving the bridesmaids, you will definitely need ribbons on the car, which you tie on from the wing mirrors to the centre of the bonnet. You can buy wedding ribbons from a florist or haberdasher. The bride may be going for wide white silk ribbon, but there's no need to go for top-of-the-range quality. You'll be surprised how much that will cost! You'll need to buy plenty, but that's already on your shopping list, too.

If you really feel like spoiling the girls, you could order a small floral arrangement to sit on the parcel shelf at the back. Alternatively, you may find that the bride has already done that, in which case you'll need to set a time to pick it up.

The ushers

Since you are in charge of the ushers, you will need to make sure they know where they are going and how and when to get there, so it's worth printing out a few extra copies of your maps so you can send them to the ushers – or simply e-mail them – when you get to those jobs (Countdown Day 14). They'll need to know about parking too.

To the honeymoon

Your final transport job is to help the groom to organise the transport for himself and his wife to leave the reception.

If they are being picked up by taxi, make sure he has booked it for the right time and place. Job done.

If you are driving them to the airport or honeymoon hotel, you will have already done what was necessary and your car will be at the reception ready. Don't forget that you cannot drink and drive, so it will be a 'dry' reception for you. Is that the best option?

If the groom is driving himself, it'll be a 'dry' reception for him. Again, that may not be a favourite idea. If he is driving, it's up to you to liaise with him to make arrangements for his car to be parked at the reception venue in advance. Do it the day before if you can; make the plans with him and write it in your diary. If the car is going to be left at a hotel, for example, overnight, do call them and check their clamping policy, just in case they only allow patrons to park overnight in their car park. They are sure to allow you to park there, but you may need to book the registration number with them in advance. If the only place to park is a public car park, make sure you abide by the ticketing rules; if the car has to be parked on a road, choose the safest place you can and it is probably best to get up early and park it there on the day of the wedding.

Whatever the arrangements, you'll be checking that all the honeymoon luggage and documents are where they are meant to be on Countdown Day 10.

What if the car won't start?

I very much doubt if the nightmare scenario of finding your car with a flat tyre or turning the key and hearing nothing but a click happens more than once in a blue moon, but nonetheless it's worth taking precautions.

You won't have time to call out the breakdown service. You won't want to change a wheel in your Armani suit. There are, however, a couple of back-up systems. Depending on the reliability of your car, you could put one or both of them in place, should the worst happen.

Chat to your next-door neighbour, brother, flatmate – someone who lives nearby and who could change a wheel – and offer them a few drinks if they clean up their car and make sure they are around just until you set off for the ceremony, so they could either help out or donate their car for the day. Check in advance that your insurance covers you, just in case.

Call round some reliable local taxi firms now and ask them the estimated arrival time at your location at the time and day in question. Programme into your mobile the numbers of the two who give you the best response times. You might even want to tell them that if you do have to ring, there's a big tip in it if they get there in record time (speed limits permitting, of course).

Today's top tip: what about winter weddings?
If you've ever left the house to go to an important early meeting at work in February and forgotten to allow time to de-ice the car, you'll know what I mean! For a wedding at any time when there is a possibility of ice or frost, add an extra 10 minutes to your getting-ready time, switch on the engine, screen heaters and fans and allow the car time to warm up and defrost before you set off.

Countdown Day 15

The Rehearsal of the Ceremony

Today's task
- Attend the ceremony rehearsal and use the occasion to make sure you are fully clued-up on what will happen on the actual day.

Why do I need to do that?
- Practice makes perfect – and knowing what is going to happen will help you enjoy it more.

What to do
- Turn up, listen – and ask questions now.

What not to do
- Doze off during the important bits.

The rehearsal

The idea of the rehearsal is to get everyone together and do a dry run of what will happen on the day. You'll have the chance to meet any members of the wedding party you haven't yet met and it's a great opportunity to ask any questions that you need to ask to clarify what you – or anybody else – should be doing on the day. From your point of view, it's the ideal opportunity to make sure you know exactly what you are expected to do at the ceremony.

At the register office

You won't actually have a rehearsal for a register office wedding and there is no formal role for the best man, but I've included a run-down of the ceremony here so you know what to expect.

Generally only close family and friends attend the wedding itself, as space is limited and it is only a short ceremony. All the guests congregate in the register office about 10 minutes before the ceremony is due to start. You should be there with the groom a little earlier, as he will need to pay any fees due and check that the information he has provided to the Superintendent Registrar is correct. Make sure you get him there on time as they have to stick to strict schedules.

Once all the guests have congregated, the ceremony begins. The Superintendent Registrar explains the legal basis for marriage, the bride and groom each makes a declaration that they are free to marry and they exchange vows and rings. The couple and two witnesses sign the register.

At the church

You and the groom arrive about 30 minutes before the ceremony is due to begin, a few minutes after the ushers and before the bulk of the guests. Check that they know what they are doing. If the groom has not paid the fees for the church, choir, bell-ringers, organist and so on, he will usually do so before the service, or ask you to deal with it.

The photographer may be there to take a couple of shots of you and the groom before you take your seats at the front, right-hand side of the church. Check the position of any heating vents in the floor so you can avoid them! Make a final check that the rings are in your pocket. There will often be music played while the guests arrive and are shown to their seats by the ushers. The last guest to arrive will be the bride's mother, so when she is escorted to her seat on the front left-hand pew, then it's all about to start.

The bridesmaids will be waiting outside for the bride and her father to arrive. The processional music will then strike up and everyone stands up. The groom will take a step forward to stand at the chancel steps, and you stand just behind and to his right. The minister will be standing on the chancel steps.

Some people think it's the bride's prerogative to be late. Most ministers think it's inconvenient, because it messes up their busy schedule. I think it's just rude! However, if, by any chance, the bride is *very* late, go outside and ring the bride's home to find out why.

The bride will be escorted down the aisle on the right arm of her father – or whoever is giving her away – followed by the bridesmaids. If she is wearing a veil, the chief bridesmaid will rearrange it off her face and take her bouquet. There is usually a hymn, then everyone sits down except the bride and her father and you and the groom.

The minister will ask if anyone knows any reason why the marriage should not take place. Assuming the groom's brother doesn't stand up(!), the minister asks who is giving the bride away. Her father places the bride's right hand in the minister's, who gives it to the groom. Her father then sits down next to his wife. The groom and then the bride make their vows. The minister will then ask for the rings and you then place them on the Bible that he offers to you. He will bless the rings, which will then be exchanged. The minister will then pronounce the couple man and wife. This is the 'You may now kiss the bride' bit. They may go up to the altar rail for prayers.

The service will follow with a short talk by the minister, one or two hymns, or perhaps a psalm, and some prayers. Since each service differs, the minister will tell you what to do and invite you to sit down or stand, as appropriate. From now on, you do what the congregation does and don't follow the groom up to the altar!

At the end of the ceremony, the wedding party – including you – will either go to the vestry or to a side table to sign the register. If you have been asked to be a witness, you will sign as such but it is usually the two fathers who fulfil that role. The certificate is given to the groom. The congregation usually sing a hymn or listen to someone singing while this is going on. The photographer is usually allowed to take a photograph.

Triumphal music strikes up and it's all done! The bride and groom walk back down the aisle, followed by the bridesmaids in pairs. You offer your left arm to the chief bridesmaid and follow them down the aisle. Keep a reasonable distance from whoever is in front as the bride and groom are likely to walk slowly and stop and smile as they see special guests in the congregation. If you are directly behind the bride and groom, be especially careful to keep a pace or two away from the train on her dress, if she has one. The groom's father will join the procession escorting the bride's mother, then the bride's father with the groom's mother, followed by the guests.

The photographer may take a photograph of the recessional, but he will really click into gear when you get outside. He will have a set list of what photographs he wants to take: bride and groom; bride and groom with best man and bridesmaids; bride's family, and so on. You can be a help in getting the right people to the right place when he wants them.

When that is over, it's confetti time and the bride and groom are waved off to the reception. You may then drive the bridesmaids, or just go with the wedding party. Before you go, make sure the chief usher knows he has to be the last to leave and make sure everyone is safely on their way to the reception and nothing – and no one – has been left behind.

Other wedding venues

Civil weddings can now take place at a variety of registered venues, and they tend to be slightly longer than a simple register office wedding, with more guests and more of a personal input from the bride and groom. They may therefore have secular readings or music, for example, making them more like a church service in structure. Since they do vary so much, you'll need to chat through the sequence with the bride and groom so you know what to expect on the day. Most couples will start with the traditional ceremony structure in mind, so if you know what to expect from a church wedding, you are likely to find that is transferred in a similar form to the secular location.

Today's top tip: the rings

As far as the ceremony is concerned, having the rings ready at the right moment is the most important responsibility for you. Decide in advance which pocket you are going to put them in and don't change your mind. Especially if it's a brand-new suit, make sure the pocket has been unstitched beforehand and check it for holes – even if the suit is brand-new! The last thing to do before you leave the house is check that the rings are in your pocket. After that, reassure yourself from time to time by patting the pocket on the outside. There is no reason to take them out until you are safely in the church and about to hand them over. You should certainly never take them out when you are on the move, outside on a gravel path or near a drain!

Countdown Day 14

Are the Ushers
Up to Speed?

Today's task
- Check that the ushers know all the details of what is expected of them.

Why do I need to do that?
- You are in charge of making sure that the ushers know their job and do it well.

What to do
- You should have sorted out all the details with the groom by now so all you need to do is make sure you pass the information on to the ushers.

What not to do
- Assume they have worked everything out for themselves.

Who are they?

As we said at the beginning, the ushers are usually the groom's and bride's brothers and close friends. There is usually a chief usher and one usher for every 50 or so guests. There are no age barriers but they should be old enough to be sensible and responsible. It is best if they don't have young children to look after or other responsibilities that would make it difficult for them to do their job without distraction.

You should already have a note of all their names, telephone numbers and e-mail addresses on pages 34–5 (Countdown Day 20). You will probably already have talked to them when you organised the stag night (Countdown Day 18), and will get to know them that evening (Countdown Day 7). They don't usually attend the rehearsal, but if they are brothers of the bride or groom they may be there, too (Countdown Day 15). If all these 'you should haves' are making your nervous, that can only mean you haven't done some tasks that should have been ticked off by now. Get on with it!

Getting in touch

You can either give each of the ushers a ring to chat through what is expected of them, or a much more sociable option is to arrange to meet up for a drink and run through the day's events and their responsibilities with them in one go. If everyone is local, that is the best option as it gives you a chance to introduce everyone and break the ice before the big day. It will also save you having to say the same thing over and over again. But if everyone lives at a distance, you may have to stick with the telephone.

Either way, tick off the items you need to tell everyone so you can make sure you don't forget anything. If you are telling them all separately, tick the items off each time, otherwise you may think you've told the last guy something just because you've heard yourself say it so many times.

What should they wear?

The dress code for the wedding will already have been set (Countdown Day 17), and the same applies for the ushers as for you. If it is a formal wedding, both you and they will already know what you are wearing and arrangements to hire suits – if you don't already have them – will have been put in motion by the groom. These suits are traditionally paid for by the groom's family.

If they are wearing lounge suits, just ask them what they are wearing so you can make sure they have something suitable. They also need to be responsible for their own shirt, tie, socks, shoes and any other accessories. As with your outfit, if there is a colour scheme, the bride will already have told you about it. She may tell the ushers in order to make sure they complement the scheme, or she may not. Make sure you know and pass on any relevant information to them.

What do they need to bring?

The ushers should not need to bring anything special with them, although a mobile phone is useful as a precautionary measure, just in case anything goes wrong and you need to get in touch. Make sure you give your mobile phone number to all the ushers and that they programme it into their handsets. You should already have their numbers in your phone, if not do it now so you don't have to remember any contact numbers in case of any last-minute changes of plan.

They could also pop a large umbrella in their car, as if everyone is well provided with umbrellas, it is much less likely to rain! For a formal occasion, it should be black, but if it stops them ruining their brand-new outfit even before they get to the church, I think most guests won't worry too much!

What do ushers do?

The ushers are your back-up team, supporting you and helping to make sure the day goes smoothly. You or the groom can give them specific jobs if that is helpful, or ask them to perform particular tasks during the course of the day.

It's up to you to check out what needs to be done and instruct them accordingly.

At the ceremony

- The ushers should be the first to arrive at the ceremony venue, aiming to get there about 40 minutes before it is due to start. It's crucial that they all arrive on time.

- If there are buttonholes and corsages for the wedding party, they may already have been delivered to the venue, or you will bring them when you arrive 10 or so minutes later. The ushers make sure they are distributed to the wedding party as they arrive. Buttonholes are usually provided for the ushers as well.
- As the guests begin to arrive, one or more of the ushers can help to supervise the parking, if that is necessary.
- You will also have made sure the order-of-service sheets are ready at the church, and the ushers hand out these and the hymn books to the guests as they arrive. They should place a few on the front pews for the family and wedding party.
- Most churches only allow a few official photographs at the ceremony, so you can ask the ushers to mention this discreetly to anyone wielding a camera or camcorder. The same applies to confetti, although most people are sensible enough to buy rice-paper confetti nowadays. You can also ask them to request that mobile phones be switched off.
- It is the ushers' job to escort or direct guests to their seats for the ceremony. If it's a formal wedding, they should offer their left arm to each lady and escort them; the lady's partner will follow behind. The bride's family and friends sit in the seats or pews on the left-hand side and

the groom's family on the right. The front pews are reserved for the wedding party and the rows behind for close family.

- Do let the ushers know if there are any special arrangements, for example if either of the sets of parents is divorced. Traditionally, if they are not remarried, they sit together; if they are remarried, they sit with their new partners, but this is a matter for individual decisions.
- Tell them to guide families with young children to seats from which they can make a hasty exit if necessary.
- The last guest to arrive is the bride's mother. The chief usher escorts her to her seat, then all the ushers take their seats at the back of the church. If anyone arrives late, one of the ushers should greet them and escort them to a pew at the back as quietly as possible.

After the ceremony
- The ushers can help the photographer to organise the guests for the photographs.
- Once the bride and groom have departed for the reception, the ushers should help to make sure everyone has transport to the venue and that no one is left behind.
- The ushers are supposed to escort the bridesmaids throughout the day. In our less-formal times this is not always necessary but, with any luck, could be more of a pleasure than a chore!

- They often help by offering lifts to any guests who do not have their own transport to the reception.
- The ushers check that no one has left anything at the ceremony venue and the chief usher should be the last to leave for the reception.

At the reception

- Again, one or more of the ushers can help out with parking arrangements if necessary.
- They may be asked to distribute drinks as people arrive at the reception, help with taking coats to the cloakroom or showing people to their seats.
- It is very helpful if they circulate during the reception and help to make sure everyone is enjoying themselves and does not need any special attention. If any guests have any special needs, one of the ushers can be designated to look after them.
- If there are younger guests – particularly young bridesmaids or page boys – some of the ushers could be asked to organise some games for them, or keep them amused and happy during the speeches or at any other moments when time is likely to drag. They could perhaps come armed with a bag of colouring books and crayons, or there may be somewhere to show a suitable video for half an hour, perhaps during the speeches.

Timing and transport

The ushers need to arrive at the ceremony venue about 40 minutes early, so they need clear directions on where it is and how to get there. You will already have sorted out your own route, maps and transport, so it's just a question of passing on that information. Don't forget to tell them anything they need to know about parking arrangements.

Especially if it's a church with a common name in a large town, make sure they are clear which one it is. You can send or e-mail them a copy of your map, or direct them to www.multimap.com to get their own. You can pass on any information about special events on the day or road problems, so they can ensure they leave enough time to get there.

Ask them if they mind giving a lift to the reception to anyone who does not have their own transport. As long as that's okay, tactfully remind them to vacuum and wash the car as it would be embarrassing to have to empty the muddy rugby kit off the back seat before the passengers can get in – and it's bound to be the guest in the cream suit.

Help! I can't be in two places at once

If there are any jobs you have been asked to do – such as collecting the order-of-service sheets to take to the church – and you can't manage it, just call the chief usher, or one of the other ushers, and ask them to deputise for you.

Today's top tip: the perfect escort

If you or the ushers do have to escort a lady on the day, remember to offer her your left arm. The way to remember this is that this leaves your sword arm free to protect her! If any of you is left-handed, that's tough, I'm afraid, as you weren't allowed to be left-handed when they established these traditions!

Countdown Day 13
Write Your Speech

Today's task
- Make a first draft of your speech.

Why do I need to do that?
- You need to make a short speech at the reception and a good one will help to make the occasion. A bad one, on the other hand...

What to do
- Think about it, make lots of notes, then put together a first draft.

What not to do
- Leave it until later.

Do I have to do it now?

Unless you are an accomplished speaker, the prospect of giving a public speech can be – and usually is – daunting. If you are an accomplished speaker you will already know that it takes time, hard work and preparation to give a speech that sounds fluent and unscripted. You will already have started work long ago.

On the fairly safe assumption therefore that anyone who needs this chapter is not so fortunate, you really need to give yourself as much time as possible to draft out your speech, revise it and practise it. Don't leave it any longer; you are already cutting it fine as it is. Remember: it only has to be three minutes long, thoughtful and sincere. No one is expecting a professional stand-up routine. You are perfectly capable of making an honest, amusing and endearing three-minute best man's speech that everyone will applaud. Have confidence in yourself.

What do I have to say?

You come on after the bride's father and the groom, who finishes his speech by proposing a toast to the bridesmaids. You reply on behalf of the bridesmaids, thanking the groom for his compliments and paying the girls some of your own.

It's then your job to say a few words about the groom, by way of introducing him to the bride's extended family and friends. You may have a few amusing but tasteful anecdotes, an appropriate joke or perhaps you'd prefer just a few well-chosen descriptive compliments.

You then read out any telemessages or cards, usually just a small selection from significant family or friends who have not been able to come to the wedding.

Finally, you tell the guests what will happen for the rest of the evening and announce the cutting of the cake.

You may also have to act as master of ceremonies to introduce the other speakers and let the guests know what is going on. All that is covered in the next chapter.

When do I have to say it?

Tomorrow we'll also go through the sequence of who says what at the reception, so all that will become clear then. For the moment, just concentrate on your own speech.

What is suitable ... and what is not?

Remember that you are talking to a family audience and that you are recommending your best friend to his new relations and friends. You are there to build rapport, not to be divisive. You want to make people smile, not blush or be offended.

- Never swear, blaspheme, or include any stories or jokes that might upset anyone, including the children. This is a pre-watershed occasion.
- Don't say anything that would embarrass your friend, except in the gentlest and most friendly way.
- Never mention other relationships and certainly don't stray into sexual prowess.
- Never give away any secrets or say anything that is not meant to be made public.
- Don't mention family arguments or divorces.

- Don't try to make fun of anyone.
- Never express doubts about the relationship.
- Only make positive compliments about the bride.
- Don't refer to anything sad.
- Don't be patronising.

Apart from that, you can say what you like! If you are in doubt about whether something should be included, it shouldn't – cut it out. It's that simple.

How do I start?

Start either with a large pad of paper and a pen, or a computer. Obviously if you are happy working on screen it makes drafting and redrafting easier. Choose whichever you are most comfortable with. If you are on a computer, do make sure you save the document when you start and maintain a regular back-up save while you are working on it.

Jot down the following headings, which cover the main sections of the speech. If you are writing on paper, start a separate sheet for each one.

- The bridesmaids.
- The groom.
- Anecdotes.
- Telemessages and cards.
- What happens next.
- Cutting the cake.

Write down in any order and as roughly as you like, words, phrases, sentences or anything you can think of on those topics that relate to the occasion. It doesn't matter if you have loads of ideas for one section. It doesn't matter if you are not sure if they are suitable. They don't have to be proper stories or anecdotes. Just scribble everything down in rough note form at this stage. Sorting it out will come later. Here are some ideas to help you get going.

The bridesmaids

You are looking for a few sincere words of thanks to the groom and some well-chosen compliments to the bridesmaids. If you find out what the groom is going to say, that will make it easier to respond. You must make sure your comments are suitable to the ages of the bridesmaids as obviously you are going to flatter a five-year-old with quite a different compliment than an 18-year-old. If you don't have children, ask the advice of someone who does – you can always try your mum. Find out what they are interested in as that might give you some clues. Always make sure you get the names right.

- Names.
- Ages if they are young.
- Relationships to the bride.
- Where they have travelled from, if it is a long distance.
- A few complimentary words you feel comfortable with: stunning, pretty, energetic, lively, beautiful, happy.

- A few gentle hints that they'd make great partners, too.
- That you are looking forward to dancing with all of them later in the evening.

If there are page boys, you need to thank them as well but do it separately from the bridesmaids and take a more 'matey' approach. Especially if they are school age, it's quite possible they are slightly embarrassed about the whole thing so you can reassure them that it's okay.

The groom

This should aim to explain how you know the groom, to fit you into the picture and to give a potted description of him: what you might put down if you had to describe him in 10 words or less.

- How long you've known him.
- How much you value his friendship.
- Some words you might use to describe him: extrovert, funny, caring, reliable.

Anecdotes

Light-weight humour comes next. The ideal story to include is an amusing anecdote that reveals what a nice guy he is and what a great husband he'll make. You could also include something to show how his relationship has changed him – for the better.

- How you and the groom first met.
- A schoolboy occasion.
- Any sporting achievements.

- When he first met his wife and his initial reaction (wow factor).
- Something that shows how well suited they are and suggests they will enjoy a long and happy marriage.

Telemessages and cards

By definition, you will only be able to fill this out at the last minute. The best person to help is usually the bride's mother, who generally takes charge of special messages.

- Only read out a couple of messages from relatives or special friends who have not been able to come to the wedding. There may be an aunt in Australia or a school friend in Thailand.
- Don't repeat 'Good wishes for your health and happiness from…' over and over again – everyone will go to sleep.

What happens next

For the final section, find out the format for the rest of the entertainment so you can pass that information on to the guests. For example, you might ask everyone to move through to another room once the cake-cutting is over, or suggest they move to one side of the room while the tables are cleared so that the dancing can begin. If it's an informal occasion, you could request volunteers.

Cutting the cake

This is simply to announce that the bride and groom will cut the cake. It will probably already be on the top table or a convenient side table. The cake-cutting will be accompanied by applause and photographs, and you can then simply close the proceedings by saying something like: 'Thank you, everyone. Please enjoy the rest of the evening.'

Shaping it into a speech

Once you have all these notes, you need to begin to select what you are going to use and what you are going to discard. Again, you may still be unsure which anecdotes will work until you write them up. That's not a problem. Just keep them on the list until the next stage.

You then need to write up the text you have chosen. Try to make it sound natural, so use your usual style of language, and remember that you are going to be speaking out loud, not reading silently, so if you can read it aloud as you work up the text, you'll start to feel whether or not particular sections work. Don't use long and involved words or sentences that could trip you up. A fun tongue-twister might seem a good idea in advance but is likely to tie both your tongue and your stomach in knots at the prospect of pulling it off in front of 100 people.

Remember that professional speeches take a lot of hard work and are drafted and redrafted many times until they work. Small changes can make a big difference.

Writer's block

If you are really struggling and just can't think of anything, start with the easy bits: the names of the bridesmaids, where you first met the groom, what sports he plays or hobbies he enjoys, which football team he supports. When you have put down all the factual stuff, leave it alone for a bit.

Go for a run, make a cup of coffee, do anything but stare at the page or the computer screen for half an hour. Then go and dig out something that will jog some memories: photo albums, match programmes, university club membership cards, anything to do with your past. They may well remind you of some funny anecdotes featuring the groom.

If that fails, go for the favourite fall-back. Assuming she knows the groom, ring your mum and ask how she would describe him and if she has any memories that are revealing about him. If that's not an option, what about mutual friends? All you are looking for is something that will spark your own imagination and get you started.

In any event, you may well think of new or better ideas during the next few days, so jot them down and see if you can work them into the speech. You sometimes have the best ideas in the bath or when you are thinking about something completely different. Don't try to include everything. If two stories illustrate the same personality trait, then one has to go.

Try it out

When you have something that seems to work reasonably well, read it out loud and see how long it takes. If it sounds reasonable, and is somewhere around the three to 10 minutes mark, save it and then leave it alone for a few days before you come back to it.

On Countdown Day 8, I'll tell you all you need to know about how to polish it, how to remember it and how to deliver it.

Today's top tip: beware the thesaurus

You can use a thesaurus to help give you ideas and think of neat ways of expressing yourself, but don't use words you would not normally use just because you think they sound impressive. They won't. You could even use them in slightly the wrong context and sound ignorant. You are looking for a conversational and natural speech that will sound sincere. If you cram in fancy words that are not part of your normal vocabulary, you'll just sound silly.

Countdown Day 12

Get Clued Up about the Reception

Today's task
- Make sure you know what happens at the reception.

Why do I need to do that?
- This is the part that contains your speech, as well as the fun stuff.

What to do
- Read this chapter and chat to the bride and groom, if necessary.

What not to do
- Assume it's just one big party. It will be, but there are likely to be formal bits, too.

Variety is the spice of weddings

This is the part of the day that is likely to be the most personal, in a way, as it should be the party that the bride and groom and their family will most enjoy. The style of the wedding will almost certainly follow through into the style of the reception, so if it has been an up-market, top-hat-and-tails affair, then you can expect a formal dinner; for a civil wedding it may be a buffet and a disco. You'll need to ask the groom what sort of occasion it is and how it is going to be organised. The outline below errs on the side of formality so makes a good starting point for a customised reception plan.

The receiving line

At a formal reception, you will be among the first to arrive and will join the bride and groom and both sets of parents to welcome the guests; this is known as the receiving line. You may join the end of the line with the chief bridesmaid, or you may have to act as master of ceremonies or toastmaster and introduce the guests as they arrive. If that's the case, stand just before the line, quietly ask the guests' names as they come up to you, then as they walk up to the line announce them as:

- Mr and Mrs Peter Wilkinson (for a married couple);
- Mr Michael Smythe and Mrs, Miss or Ms Sandra Wilson (for an unmarried couple);
- Mr John Green, Miss Sarah Wormsley, Mrs Susan Howard or Ms Helena Wheatley (for a person on their own).

If there are likely to be lords and ladies present, you ought to do a bit more homework and find out the proper modes of address for specific titles. If you haven't done that, just repeat exactly what they tell you.

On less formal occasions, you may be asked to offer drinks, take charge of coats, or generally make sure guests know where to go when they arrive. Ask the ushers to help.

Deputise one of the ushers to watch out for anyone who has arrived with a gift, so they can take the present to a safe side table in the reception area, where the bride and groom can open them later if there is time. If there are young bridesmaids, they would also enjoy helping with this. Security is key here. Make sure no unwanted visitors can help themselves and that the bride's mum will collect everything at the end.

Time to eat

Once everyone has arrived, there will be a signal for the wedding breakfast – as the first meal the couple enjoy together is called. If you are the toastmaster, you may be asked to announce the meal by saying something like: 'Ladies and gentlemen, please be seated as dinner is now being served.' You may be asked to help people to find their seats, or just to encourage the ushers to do so.

Your place will be on the top table. The usual sequence, looking at the table and going from left to right, is: chief bridesmaid, groom's father, bride's mother, groom, bride, bride's father, groom's mother, then you – the best man.

Especially if the minister has come to the reception, he or she should be seated at the end of the top table. He will be asked to say grace, so when everyone is seated, you would say: 'Ladies and gentlemen, please could we have silence for Reverend Jones who will now say grace.'

A word about the wine. If you have got this far you will be feeling really good about how well it has gone to this point and beginning to realise that speech-time is almost upon us. That combination is bound to encourage anyone to enjoy to a few glasses of wine. Obviously you want to enjoy your meal and relax with your friends – and perhaps build up a little Dutch courage while you are at it – but do keep it to just one or two glasses. One of the biggest social dangers with alcohol is that it makes you think you can do things when you can't! Don't risk it!

The speeches

At the end of the meal, it's time for the speeches. The host or the caterers should make sure people's glasses are charged at this point. If that hasn't happened, a tactful reminder might be in order. It's embarrassing for guests to stand up to a toast with an empty glass. It's also a good time to make sure you have a glass of water to hand and to nip to the toilet.

Find out beforehand whether or not there will be

microphones. If there are, think about the logistics of passing the stands down the table so the cables don't become tangled. Unless there is a separate toastmaster, it is a good idea to take on that role, then everyone knows what is going on. It is very unsettling if people are not sure whether it's their turn next and there will be a fair few nerves flying around at this stage.

You should stand and tap a glass with a spoon, then wait for the hubbub to settle down before you say something like: 'Ladies and gentlemen, welcome to this afternoon's celebrations. I would like to introduce the bride's father, Mr John Smith.' You sit down, and the bride's father will stand to talk about his daughter, welcome his new son-in-law to the family, thank the guests for coming to the wedding and propose a toast to the bride and groom. You should stand up as a signal for everyone else to stand for the toast. There will then be quite a lot of chair-scraping and muttering while they all take their seats again.

You should remain standing so that when the noise has died down you can introduce the groom: 'Ladies and gentlemen, the groom, Mr Simon Wilson.' Sit down when the groom stands. He will thank his father-in-law for his comments, tell the guests how happy he is to be married to his new wife, thank the hosts for a wonderful wedding and anyone else who merits a special mention. He will thank everyone for coming and for their gifts, and finally thank the attendants and propose a toast to them.

You remain standing. This is your bit and you have already made a great start in putting your speech together so you know what happens here. Once the cake has been cut, it's time to party.

In the unlikely event that anyone dries up during the speeches, you might just have to jump in and wing it. You may just want to thank them and continue with the toast, or perhaps you could have a light-hearted comment about what a special day it is so that you can fill the void.

Dance the night away

The bride and groom usually choose the opening number and take the floor together, usually to applause. When the song is just over half way through, you take the chief bridesmaid on to the floor to join the dancing. The groom's father will ask the bride's mother, and the bride's father will ask the groom's mother. Once the main wedding party are on the floor, it's well and truly under way.

You should make a point of dancing with each of the bridesmaids, the bride's mother and the groom's mother during the course of the evening. As well as the young and beautiful guests, spare a thought for the 'old' aunties who'd love a turn around the dance floor. They'll love to be asked. You'll need to explain to your girlfriend *before* the event that it's part of your duties, and make sure she is sitting with other friends.

You can also make yourself generally sociable to help the party go with a swing. Since everyone will know who you are, it is easy to approach any of the guests who look lost or are stuck on their own. Everyone will be talking about the wedding so there are plenty of opening lines that will get a conversation going. Just introduce yourself and ask them something that you think will interest them:

- Are you related to John or Mary?
- What an excellent band; do you like this kind of music?
- Doesn't Mary look lovely?
- Wasn't the weather wonderful for the occasion?
- Did you have far to come?
- Have you known them for long?
- What a delicious meal!

I'm sure you can do much better than that!

Keep an eye out for bride and groom 'monopolisers'. The happy couple will want to talk with as many of their guests as possible and there are always one or two who try to keep them talking for too long. Go up to them with a polite interruption and either take over the conversation so the bride or groom can slip away, or tell them that their boss is desperate to have a minute's chat and could you drag them away. The bride's parents might well appreciate a similar service, too.

Young children

A wedding reception is a very exciting place for young children and there's plenty to do, so the chances are they will have a wonderful time and not begin to wear out until long after everyone else has slowed down. Older cousins tend to gravitate towards the younger ones to look after them, too. However, if you and the ushers can keep an eye on the children, it will relieve the pressure on the parents and be much appreciated. If it is a very long reception, you might be able to organise an 'interval' of cartoons on DVD or video with juice and a biscuit or something so they can recharge their batteries. Small children are likely to become fractious if they have to go too long without food – a probem you can easily prevent.

The wedding gifts

It used to be the case that a display of the wedding gifts was arranged at the reception; now it is more often done separately as a display of the contents of the couple's new home is not always the best security idea. If there is a display, the bride's mother will probably have organised it but she won't want to worry about it during the reception. You can offer to keep an eye on it, or ask the ushers to show people where it is if necessary. You'll need to check out if this is part of your brief.

Preparing to leave

During the course of the reception, you and the ushers and bridesmaids slip away to decorate the couple's going-away car. When you do your shopping (Countdown Day 9), you'll find decorations are already on your shopping list. Here are some ideas to start you off.

● Tin cans on string to tie to the bumper.
● Confetti to sprinkle in the car or put into the glove box.
● Parcel ribbon or streamers to tie to the wing mirrors.
● Balloons on strings to tie to the aerial.

Never interfere with the mechanics of the car, use lipstick or shaving foam (or anything similar) on the paintwork, or obscure the windows. They will need to drive the car for a short distance at least.

You could also be super-helpful and put a few cleaning-up items in a plastic bag in the boot:

● A couple of cloths.
● A small pair of scissors.
● A dustbin bag for the rubbish.

When the couple are almost ready to leave, they will go and change. You should take charge of the groom's wedding suit and make sure it is taken safely home or returned to the hire company. You should also make sure the car is loaded with their luggage and that they have all the honeymoon documents.

It is quite popular to have a leave-taking line where all the male guests line up on one side and the females opposite them in a queue leading towards the door, with the close family nearest the door. The bride goes down the male side and the groom down the female side, thanking and saying goodbye to the guests, until they are finally waved off on their way to their honeymoon.

The party may wind up at that point or it may carry on. Once it does finish, you can help to make sure all the guests leave safely and give a hand with the clearing up. Don't forget to thank the hosts for a great event and to congratulate them on a splendid occasion.

Today's top tip: don't drink and speak
Use the 'don't drink and drive' principle before you deliver your speech and you'll be sure you are on top form to give a well-delivered and entertaining speech.

Countdown Day 11
Learn to Waltz

Today's task
- Learn a few traditional dance steps.

Why do I need to do that?
- You won't be able to avoid dancing and it's a lot more stylish than shuffling.

What to do
- Ask someone to teach you some basic steps.

What not to do
- Tread on anyone's toes.

Face the music

The opening number of the dancing will be chosen by the bride and groom, and it is usually a slow romantic waltz, as befits the occasion. You and the chief bridesmaid will have to join them on an almost empty dance floor. If you can at least move round with a little style, you'll feel far more comfortable about the experience – and you may even impress that gorgeous bridesmaid!

During the evening, you should try to dance with as many people as you can, and for this kind of occasion, the music is usually a mixture of styles to keep everyone happy, from the latest chart hits to '70s glam-rock, '60s retro, and a few ballroom classics for the olds. If you can recognise a waltz and take some of the older ladies on to the floor, they'll feel far more comfortable than trying to wriggle in a bizarre fashion to some hip-hop number.

Who's going to help?

You could book a one-off ballroom dancing lesson at a local dance school to solve your problem but perhaps that's a bit extreme for most.

For the DIY option, it used to be the case that anyone with a few grey hairs would know the basics of ballroom dancing. That's no longer true. To be fairly sure they can help, you need to ask someone who was born before the Beatles. Scary thought, isn't it? So your grandma is more likely to be able to help than your mum. Alternatively, some youngsters take ballroom dancing as a hobby, so you might have a cousin, sister or neighbour who can help you out.

If you know the chief bridesmaid and she is as ignorant as you about this, she might be game for learning with you so you can really look good on the dance floor.

If all else fails, push the chairs back, pick up a cushion, set up the CD and get on the floor!

One, two, three

A waltz has a simple one-two-three rhythm that's easy to recognise. Get hold of 'Come Away with Me' by Norah Jones. It's perfect to learn to. Listen to the music and you will hear a slight emphasis on the first beat: **one**-two-three. You can start straight away with the music, or learn the steps first, if you prefer. If you want a more detailed explanation, visit www.dancetv.com or www.ballroomdancers.com.

Stand face to face with your partner so that she is looking over your right shoulder. Place your right hand just beneath her left shoulder blade with your arm slightly out. She will place her left hand on your shoulder. Raise your left arm to about her eye level and she will place her right hand lightly in it. You will be moving forward and your partner will be moving back, so it's up to you to lead her where you want her to go, and make sure she doesn't bump into anyone.

Listen to the music and feel the rhythm, then take your first step on the emphasised beat, and keep in time with the music.

- Step forward on your left foot.
- Step forward on your right foot so your feet are slightly apart.
- Bring your left foot next to your right foot.
- Step forward on your right foot.

4

3

7

2

6

1

5

- Step forward on your left foot so that your feet are slightly apart.
- Bring your right foot next to your left foot.

Your partner will mirror your steps on the opposite feet. That's all there is to it. Just practise staying with the music and you can work your way round the floor.

If you were dancing properly, of course, you would then learn how to turn corners. That is beyond the scope of this exercise! Simply guide your partner in a gentle curve round the corner as you are dancing towards it, rather than staying in a straight line all the time.

What's the alternative?

If you know for a fact that the opening number is Iron Maiden and the music will only get heavier, then there are a number of alternative options on using today's planning time.

- On a musical theme, burn a CD or record a tape of all the bride and groom's favourite dance music to take along to the reception for the DJ to play.
- Burn a CD or record a tape of their favourite romantic music to leave in the going-away car.
- Work on your speech.
- Memorise the names of all the wedding party.
- Check through the events of the day and personalise them for your specific occasion.
- Start thinking about wedding-gift shopping ideas.

- Order a bunch of flowers or a bottle of champagne to be sent to the host and hostess on the day after the wedding to thank them for a great time.

Today's top tip: mark your card
If you don't know the origin of this rather odd expression, it comes from the days when ladies would have a dance card and the gentlemen would actually book dances with them! If you can dance with as many of the guests as you can, it's a great way of helping to get the party going, mixing people up and helping them to enjoy themselves, too.

Countdown Day 10

Are You Ready for the Honeymoon?

Today's task
- Find out exactly how much help you need to give the groom to get everything ready for the honeymoon.

Why do I need to do that?
- It's your job to have the luggage and documents ready when the couple leave the reception.

What to do
- Talk to the bride and groom and make the necessary arrangements.

What not to do
- Assume the groom will do everything himself.

Why should I worry about the honeymoon?

You obviously won't have a great deal to do with the honeymoon arrangements but it is your job to make sure that the honeymoon luggage for both the bride and groom is ready at the reception for when they go away. Since you are supposed to be his right-hand man, it might be helpful to check through with him that he has all the necessary paperwork and documents, while you are making the luggage arrangements, as there is still a little time left to fill in any gaps. If he is busy, you may be able to offer to take on some tasks for him.

The wedding night and the honeymoon

First you need to establish exactly what the couple plan to do after the wedding.

- They may be staying the night in the hotel where they are holding the reception so they don't have to leave the party early.
- They may be going on to another hotel for the night then going away the following day.
- They may be going home and saving their holiday until a later date.
- They may be going straight to the airport.

Obviously what they need to take and where their luggage should be will be determined by their plans, so make a few notes so that you have all the information you need.

First-night hotel . . . .
Telephone . . . .
E-mail . . . .
Address . . . .
. . . .

Holiday flight number . . . .
Airport . . . .
Flight time . . . .
Destination . . . .
Hotel . . . .

Other holiday details . . . .
. . . .

Luggage required . . . .
. . . .

Documents required:
- Passports
- Tickets
- Currency
- Marriage certificate
- Inoculation certificates
- Insurance

The luggage

Once you have decided what they need and where they are going, you can establish where the luggage needs to be so that it is ready for them. Specify a time for everything to be ready so that you can pick it up in good time, the day before if possible.

If they are going away in the groom's car, you may be able to lock everything in the boot the day before and deliver it to the reception venue. If the reception is in a hotel, you may be able to deliver it there the day before for the hotel to keep it secure. If you do that, make sure it is clear how you will retrieve it if another member of staff is on duty. It may be easier to pack it all in your car boot and transfer it later in the day.

Obviously the documents need to be kept safe. The groom may entrust them to you at the beginning of the day, in which case you need to keep them on you, or deliver them to the hotel reception, for example, for safe-keeping.

You really need to think round what is required and come up with the best solution in the circumstances.

The going-away outfits

Most couples change out of their wedding kit before they leave and you will be in charge of making sure the groom's change of clothes is ready when he needs it. The chief bridesmaid looks after the bride. Again, a hotel reception makes this easy, as they will have a designated room. Otherwise you will have to improvise.

Today's top tip: be security conscious
A neatly packed case full of a fortnight's worth of clothes is a tempting target for an opportunist. Don't leave cases unattended anywhere insecure. It only takes a second to pick them up and walk away with them and no one will challenge someone carrying a suitcase in a hotel. Needless to say, documents are even more valuable and must be kept secure at all times.

Countdown Day 9
Retail Therapy

Today's task
- Go shopping for everything you need for the big day.

Why do I need to do that?
- You'll look really silly without a shirt and really stingy if you don't give the couple a present.

What to do
- Go with a companion if that's more efficient for you, shop online if you have time, but just do it.

What not to do
- Put it off – you don't have time for that.

Shopping tips

I have separated shopping for your suit (Countdown Day 17) from shopping for the gift and anything else you need, so those who hate shopping should already have read the tips to make it as painless as possible. Just in case you skipped them, here's a quick resumé:

- Decide what you need and make a list before you go.
- Mark potential stores on the list.
- Go early or late when the shops are less crowded.
- Ask the assistants for help if you need it.
- You won't want to go with the groom to buy his gift, but pick a helpful shopping partner unless you prefer to shop on your own.
- Only buy online if you can be absolutely sure you'll receive the goods on time.

Clothes

You should have bought these already, but if you have anything left on your clothes-shopping list, transfer it to today's list (on pages 123–5) now.

The gift

You will obviously want to buy something that your friends will really appreciate, so give this some thought before you make a decision. First, set your budget and keep to it. Then think about what sort of present you would like to give them.

Do you want to give them something for the home? If they are setting up home together for the first time that might be a good idea, but if they are combining two sets of furniture or belongings – or if they are already living together and have most of the things they need – it's not such a good idea. In that case, you might want to go for something more luxurious: crystal glasses or designer cutlery to replace a basic set. The other option, which many best men prefer, is to opt for a really personal gift. If you all have a shared interest that would be a good place to start looking for ideas. If they are keen on music, perhaps you could buy a CD player. If you really know their taste well, what about a picture? Try to narrow down the options.

Another personal and rather different idea is to go for one of the 'special days' that are now available from many department stores, speciality firms and on the net. You could buy them a champagne balloon trip, a rally-car driving session or a bungee jump! If they are the couple who already have everything, that may be just what they would like to receive.

For those of a more traditional nature, or those who can't think of anything specific they would like to buy, you'll need to find out about the wedding list. Most brides have a wedding list, which may be held at a local department store or specialist wedding-list company or by the bride or her mother. The idea is that the bride makes a list of everything the couple would like to receive. As guests make their choices from the list, that item is crossed off. Although it does seem a little calculated in some ways, it avoids duplication, ensures that the couple get what they most need and guests can be sure that their gift is appreciated. If it is well planned, there will be something for all budgets, so give the bride a ring and ask her how it is being organised so you can take a look at it, and also whether she has any preferences. She may be really keen to make up a dinner service or something – bizarre though that may sound!

Since you don't have a lot of time, it's best if whatever you do choose is something that will be relatively easy to buy. If you spend a lot of thought making the decision with such a short time left to get hold of the gift, you don't want to make it more difficult for yourself.

The wrapping

If you have chosen from a wedding-list company, they will deliver all the presents in one go. Otherwise, you will need to wrap up the present before you hand it over, so while you are at the shops buy some suitable wrapping paper, ribbon and a gift tag, and make sure you have some sticky tape. If the gift is anything large – a household item, for example – you may need more than one sheet of wrapping paper so make sure you buy enough. The rolls of wrapping paper may be the best idea. You'll need a wedding card, too. Try to choose something you think they will appreciate; they'll go on display in the bride's house for everyone to read and are likely to be kept as keepsakes after that, so if you want to go for the 'adult-humour' option, it could be best to keep it for the stag night and be more cautious in your 'public' choice!

If you know that when you put you, some wrapping paper and the simplest and most regular-shaped box in a room together, it ends up looking like World War III, it's time to enlist some help. Everyone knows whether or not they are any good at wrapping up presents, so just keep asking round your friends until you find someone who will help you out. It does make a difference to give an attractively wrapped present, so it's worth the trouble.

For the car

You'll need to check that you have car shampoo and anything else you need to smarten up the car, plus screen wash or oil if you need to top up.

You also need some sensible decorations to put on the car before the wedding: some flowers for the parcel shelf, perhaps, and certainly some ribbons for the front. You don't have to buy expensive ribbon, but do go for a thick ribbon – at least 3 cm/1½ in – for best effect.

You also will be planning to brighten up the car with decorations before the couple depart on their honeymoon, so grab some balloons and streamers or anything else that you can think of that will look good.

Finally, there's the few cleaning-up items you are going to leave in the car to help them clean up the mess you've made, so buy them while you are out if necessary.

Extras

To calm those last-minute-panic moments, it can be worth picking up a couple of cheap rings to put in your back pocket just in case of that only-in-the-movies moment when the best man can't find the rings!

You'll also want to make sure you have your own personal items: razor blades, after shave, deodorant, shampoo, comb and so on. Plus you might want some tissues (someone is bound to have forgotten, and lots of people do cry at weddings!) and mints to freshen your breath during the day.

While you are at the chemist, pick up a bottle of Bach Rescue Remedy. It's in a small brown bottle with a yellow label on the Flower Remedies counter. You might not need it, but a few drops on the tongue could be useful in calming the groom's nerves.

Do you have everything you need for the stag night: party hats, inflatable sheep…?

You might want to buy a film for your camera, or batteries if it's digital. It's unlikely you'll have a lot of time for taking photos, but you could hand it to someone else less involved and ask them to snap throughout the day.

Spend a couple of minutes thinking about anything else you might need. Run through the day before and the actual day in your mind and if there's anything at all you feel might be useful – an *A to Z* of the town, some chewing-gum, whatever – put it on the list.

The shopping list

Here's your shopping list of everything you might need to buy. Tick off anything you already have and add any extras in the spaces. Tear it out of the book so you can take it with you on your shopping trip.

Clothes

. . . .
. . . .

The gift

. . . .
. . . .

Decorations and wrapping

- Wrapping paper.
- Sticky tape.
- Wrapping ribbons or bows.
- Gift tag.
- Wedding card.
- 6 metres/6 yards white 3 cm/1½ in (or wider) florist ribbon.
- Flowers for the car.
- Balloons.
- Tin cans (not actually to buy, of course, but it's easier to keep everything on one list!).

- String.
- Confetti.
- Ribbons.
- Streamers.
- ....
- ....

For the car
- Car shampoo.
- Car polish.
- Window cleaner.
- Screen wash.
- Oil.
- ....

Clean-up kit
- Rubbish bags.
- Scissors.
- Pack of disposable cloths.
- ....

Extras
- Spare rings.
- Personal grooming items.
- ....
- ....

- Rescue Remedy.
- Packet of mints.
- ....
- Stag night props.
- ....
- Extras.
- ....
- ....
- ....

Today's top tip: I saw this and thought of you
If you put a little thought into your gift and make it really
personal – rather than just picking something off the list
at random – it will be appreciated that much more by the
bride and groom.

Countdown Day 8

Can You Hear Me at the Back?

Today's task
- Finalise your speech and practise your delivery.

Why do I need to do that?
- This is an important three minutes and you want it to go well. There are no shortcuts; the only way to ensure you can do it is to practise.

What to do
- Work on your draft and practise it out loud.

What not to do
- Chicken out.

The speech

You have already shaped your speech into pretty much how you want it. Now that you come back to it after a couple of days, you can look at it with a fresh eye. You will probably be quite impressed with it!

Read it through again, working out loud to help you test the speech and get used to how it sounds. When you make an alteration that improves something, go back to the beginning of that section and read it again. Keep going through this process until you are happy with what you have. Then read it through once more and time how long it takes. If it fulfils the following criteria, you've done it!

- It is between three and five minutes long.
- It covers the essential points: responding to the toast to the bridesmaids; introducing the groom to his new family; entertaining the guests; telemessages and special messages; explaining what is going to happen next; announcing the cutting of the cake.
- It does not contain any complicated words that could trip you up.
- It does not contain any long or involved sentences.
- It does not contain anything offensive.
- All the names are correct.

Delivery

Now you need to think about how to deliver the speech. The rules are really just common sense and a little thought will make it all feel much more natural.

You will be standing up, so make sure you can stand comfortably. Move your chair a little way away so you don't knock into it. Make sure you are not hunching your shoulders – a common sign of tension – clear your throat, take a sip of water and take a deep breath before you start.

Place your notes on the table in front of you – we'll talk more about them later – where you can see them clearly and turn the pages, if necessary. That means you can use your hands while you are speaking. If you are not someone who naturally gesticulates with your hands when talking, decide what you are going to do with them. Don't fidget with your nails, put your hands in your pockets or jingle your change. Hold them loosely together in front of you, or go for the royal option and hold them behind your back. Alternatively you could hold your notes but that does not give quite such a natural impression.

Don't try to pretend to be anyone, be yourself. Use your normal voice and accent; if you try to sound different, it won't work. Try to give a smooth performance and avoid saying 'um', 'er' or other delaying words.

You are speaking to a fairly large audience and you want them all to be able to hear you, so speak slightly louder than normal so your voice reaches easily to the back of the room. There's no need to shout. If there is a microphone, keep it just a little way away from your mouth and use your normal speaking voice.

If you look over the heads of your audience towards the people at the back, that will help to remind you that you are directing your speech right to the back of the room, and you will also be able to see if you are not quite speaking loudly enough, as they will crane towards you, look puzzled or, worst of all, give up and stop listening! If you see any of these danger signs, speak a little louder. Look slowly round the audience as you speak so they feel as though you are talking to them.

The audience want to understand every word you say, so speak clearly and just slightly more slowly than you would normally so everything is understood. Don't mumble and don't speak too quickly. At the points where you hope there will be laughter or a few comments between neighbours, be prepared to stop for a moment. Look around, watch (and enjoy) the reaction, then carry on. If you don't get the laughs naturally, don't wait for them – the pause will seem endless.

Keep a natural smile on your face. This is a happy occasion. Smiling is a two-way process so is very useful even if you are actually feeling nervous. You smile when you are happy, but if you smile, it can actually make you feel happier.

Finally, don't forget to breathe!

Practice makes perfect

Now you need to practise delivering the speech a few times. Find an empty room, have your notes on a table in front of you and imagine you are actually delivering the speech, so that you can practise your gestures and delivery as well as your speech itself. If you can do it in front of a mirror, that can be helpful. At this stage, you can still make minor changes and improvements if you find things aren't quite working or you think of new ideas. Don't start completely rewriting it at this stage. You've left it a bit late for that.

What does the team think?

Finally, it is time for some constructive criticism. This will be a nerve-racking time, but you'll probably get a really positive reaction and be pleasantly surprised. Choose one or two people you can rely on to be honest but tactful. Set up your table across the room from them and give it your best shot. Watch their reactions, keep an eye on your timing and refine your pauses to allow for their laughter. Keep in mind that you will need to pause a little longer for the laughs when you are talking to a room full of people.

If they end up really laughing, you know you are on to a winner. Otherwise judge for yourself which sections went down well and ask for their suggestions for other parts that felt a bit flat so that you can bolster them up a bit. Ask them to watch for gestures that look odd, or to tell you if you are fidgeting – you may not even have realised that you are doing it. They can also check whether your delivery is clear and sufficiently loud.

If you really can't face trying out your speech on an audience until you have come closer to finishing it, that's fine; just record it on tape and play it back to yourself first.

This will have taken quite a bit of courage and you are doing really well, so we'll leave the speech now and you can finalise it in a couple of days' time.

Today's top tip: do ask the audience
Although it will take some courage to try out your speech face to face with a friend or two, it will help you to get it right and get rid of some of your nerves. Once you know you can do it in front of an audience – however small – you'll feel more comfortable when you do it for real.

Countdown Day 7
The Stag Night

Today's task
- Make sure the groom has a seriously great night out with his best friends – and gets home in one piece.

Why do I need to do that?
- The first bit is obvious. As for the second – have you seen his fiancée when she's angry?

What to do
- Run through your plans in good time and put them into practice.

What not to do
- Get absolutely bladdered and leave him tied to a lamp-post outside the police station.

Today, you are on your own!

This is going to be the shortest section because you know perfectly well how to have a good night out and the last thing you are going to be interested in is reading up about it before you go. You need every spare minute to have a great time.

Check through that you've done everything you need to do:

- Set the format for the evening and booked any restaurant tables, if necessary.
- Invited the stags.
- Fixed the meeting time and place.
- Explained who is going to pay for what.
- Organised the kitty.
- Booked the taxis.
- Booked any other surprises, confirmed the details and either paid in advance or organised payment.
- Written your speech.
- Stocked up with hangover cures.
- Borrowed a few sleeping bags and bought something for breakfast if everyone is staying over at your place.

If you think the groom – or you – are going to be incoherent by the end of the evening, write your home address on the back of your hand – or the groom's on his hand – in felt tip pen so the taxi driver knows where to deposit you safely home. Keep a tenner in a separate pocket for the fare.

That's it – I told you I'd make it short. Have a great time! Don't forget to drink a couple of pints of water before you fall asleep – you'll feel less dehydrated in the morning.

Today's top tip: you can even earn brownie points tonight
Give the bride a quick ring before you go to reassure her that you are going to look after the groom and you haven't forgotten you are responsible for getting him safely home at the end of the evening. If you don't think you'll be able to carry off a phone call, send her a text. You could even offer to send her a text when you get him safely home if she would like you to, but in that case – whatever else you do – don't forget to send that text!

Countdown Day 6
Pamper Yourself

Today's task
- Relax, sleep, drink lots of water and look after yourself and the groom.

Why do I need to do that?
- Because you need to be sober enough to go to work tomorrow and you want to look great next weekend.

What to do
- Get your hair cut, go for the massage you booked, or just sleep.

What not to do
- Forget to get your hair cut.

Another easy day

You have another easy day ahead of you, so you can take time to recover from that great party last night, so make the most of it. Sleep in as long as you want, drink plenty of water, knock out that bad head with a couple of painkillers if you need to and get plenty of rest. With any luck, there'll be a match on the television and you can put your feet up, or just immerse yourself in the paper, a good book or your favourite CD.

Don't forget that you were in charge of whatever state the groom got into last night, so it's up to you to sort him out today – I almost said 'this morning' but I doubt if you'll see any of that.

Some people find fresh air and gentle exercise work for them, so perhaps a stroll out, a run, a swim, or a gentle workout in the gym would help get you back into shape.

Get a hair cut

You need to get your hair cut ready for the wedding at some stage soon, so today is a good day for that. Don't try anything radical just in case it doesn't work out how you planned. Go to your favourite, regular hairdresser so you can be sure you'll be happy with the results.

Some extra pampering

The girls may well be going for a facial, manicure, pedicure or something else to relax and pamper them and make them feel good. There's no reason why you shouldn't take a leaf out of their book and treat yourself to a relaxing massage, or a session in the sauna or steam room.

Today's top tip: a Great British fry-up
Many people find a full fry-up the best hangover cure, so get plenty of stocks in ready to feed yourself and your mates if they have stayed over at your place. Stock up on coffee and painkillers, too, just in case.

Countdown Day 5
Talk to the Parents

Today's task
- Get in touch with the bride's mum to check when you can collect the buttonholes and order-of-service sheets.

Why do I need to do that?
- Both need to be at the ceremony venue before everyone else arrives.

What to do
- Make a few phone calls.

What not to do
- Assume it's someone else's job.

Make that call

Even if the bride's mum – or whoever else is in charge – has made other arrangements for getting things done, she'll appreciate you getting in touch to offer your help and support.

Usually, either the best man or the chief usher collects the buttonholes and the order-of-service sheets and takes them to the church ready to distribute, the first to the wedding party and the second to the guests as they arrive.

Call up to arrange an appropriate time to pick up the necessary items, then write it in your diary. If you can't be there, delegate the job to your trusted chief usher, or to one of the other ushers. If you are lucky, one of the ushers will be the bride's brother and he can be asked to bring everything with him from the family home when he comes to the church.

You could also take the opportunity to ask whether there are any special mentions they want you to make at the end of your speech and check that they'll bring any special telemessages.

The buttonholes

These will be delivered to the family home on the morning of the wedding. The bride's mum and dad will take their buttonhole and corsage, but the remainder will have to be collected and taken to the church, for when the ushers arrive.

The order-of-service sheets

These are the running order for the service. If they are being printed, or prepared by the bride or her mum, they should be available in good time before the wedding, so you will be able to pick them up tonight, if that's easiest. Again, these need to be at the church when the ushers arrive so that each guest can be given a copy when they take their seats, so why not call round and pick them up, then drop them off with the chief usher?

How else can I help?

If you don't already know, check now whether you are driving the bridesmaids to the reception, or driving any of the wedding party or special guests. Ask any outstanding questions that relate to your responsibilities or clarify any of the details that are not clear. Don't panic anyone by giving the impression that you don't know what's going on. You are already well through your planning by now so make sure they realise that you are just being efficient and double-checking minor details.

You should use this opportunity to find out if there are any other jobs you will be expected to do between now and the wedding, or on the wedding day itself.

Have you wrapped up the gift?

Since this is an easy day on the organisation front, you can use the time to wrap up your gift for the bride and groom if you have not already done so, and write the wedding card. As I mentioned, if you know you are no good at making a present look exciting – or even passable! – ask for some help. Once the gift is ready, put it in a suitable carrier bag with the card and put it somewhere safe.

Decide when you are going to give the present to your friends. Most guests give their presents before the wedding day as it just gets too confusing if everyone is turning up with gifts on the actual day. Gifts are often exchanged between the wedding party at the rehearsal, but you weren't quite that organised by then! Chat to your mate and decide on a suitable time to hand over your gift over the next few days.

Today's top tip: offer a helping hand
As the big day looms, there are lots of little jobs that can't be done until the last minute but take up a lot of time when all added together. Ask the groom, the bride or her mum if there is anything you can do to help. You may be able to go to the printer to collect the order-of-service sheets or deliver a wedding list. They might like you to pick up an elderly relative and take her to see the wedding gifts at the bride's parents' house. It won't take up much of your time but it could take some of the pressure off the family and will be much appreciated.

Countdown Day 4
The Final Speech

Today's task
- Write or print out your speech.

Why do I need to do that?
- It will fix it in your mind and help you to deliver it really well.

What to do
- Write or print out the speech as notes, on cards or the complete speech on sheets of paper.

What not to do
- Leave it scribbled on the back of an envelope.

Which method is best for you?

There are several ways of going about preparing the notes for your speech.

You could learn the speech completely by heart and do away with notes altogether. If you are a good actor, you might like that option the best, but if you do dry up, you don't have any back-up, so it is a bit risky.

You could write out – or preferably type – the complete speech word for word and read it out. That is inclined to make it sound a little formal and stilted, and makes it difficult to inject humour and immediacy. It also means that you need to keep your eyes on your script most of the time, rather than looking at your audience, which, again, is not the most natural presentation.

The best option is usually to learn the speech by heart so that you can deliver it fluently, but have your notes in front of you as a back-up and prompt. That will give you more confidence, help your fluency and allow you a bit of ad libbing if you feel up to it.

How to make your notes

If you can type up your notes on a PC, it makes everything much easier as you can play around with the presentation before deciding how to print it out. That way you can make it as easy to read and follow as possible.

Choose a font that is easy to read: something classic and

rounded is generally the most legible for this kind of thing. Don't opt for a script face or anything complicated. Choose a fairly large font size, too, as you want to be able to leave the notes on the table in front of you and still read them clearly.

Divide up the notes into paragraphs, then break up the text with side-headings. You obviously don't have to read out the headings, but if you look down quickly at your notes, you will be able to see where you are at a glance.

You might even want to use colour, or perhaps highlighter pens, to break up the sections, or to make specific keywords stand out. Once you glance at the keyword, you'll then remember the whole paragraph. Don't use pale colours to print, though, as they don't show up well.

Once you are happy with the notes, print them out and check that you can read them easily. Number the pages clearly in the top right-hand corner so you don't get them out of order. Then print out a second set and give them to the chief bridesmaid or chief usher to take along to the wedding as a safety precaution.

Do you wear glasses?

If you wear reading glasses, make sure you test whether you need them to read your notes on the table. It may be simpler to print your notes in a larger size rather than fiddling with glasses, or looking over them at your audience and through them to see the notes.

Learn it well

If you learn your speech as well as you can, you will begin to feel really comfortable with it, and that will make your feel more relaxed and help you to deliver it well. It will also make you feel more confident so you'll loosen up and perhaps be able to add a few impromptu comments as you go along.

In any event, I'm sure it will be a great success.

Today's top tip: ask the experts
If you feel you want some more tips on writing a good speech, or some brilliant one-liners to weave into your own text, then you need a copy of *Mitch Murray's One-liners for Weddings and How to Use Them in Your Speech* (0-572-01896-7). A successful professional speechwriter and lyric writer, Mitch has been described by the late Bob Monkhouse as 'Britain's top composer of funny, funny speeches'.

Countdown Day 3
Try Out the Route

Today's task
- Check the routes and timings for the big day.

Why do I need to do that?
- It will give you the chance to do a final check on your timings and pre-empt any potential problems.

What to do
- Do a rehearsal of the drives you will have to make on the wedding day.

What not to do
- Decide how long you think it will take and then deduct 10 minutes.

Finishing touches

There's only a couple of days to go and the jobs are getting easier by the minute because you are into checking over work you've already done and putting the final finishing touches to the arrangements. Don't make the mistake of avoiding doing anything at all – there might be something you've missed.

The routes

Confirm the routes you will have to take on the wedding day.

- Your flat to the groom's flat.
- Groom's flat to the church.
- Church to the reception.

Add any others to the list; if you are taking the bride and groom to the airport, for example, or picking up the flowers from the bride's mum.

Then check that you know exactly where they all are, how to get from A to B and how long it will take.

- Do you need a map or are you familiar with the locations and the routes between them?
- How long is each leg of the journey going to take?
- Where are you going to park at each venue?
- If parking is difficult, will you need to allow extra time?
- How much time will you need to allow for collecting items or packing the car?

- Did you check for any road works or special events on the day? If not, check the local paper now to make sure it's not carnival day.

Drive the routes

It won't take you long to drive over each of the routes so you are absolutely sure everything is going to go precisely to plan on the day.

If you encounter any problems, you've still got plenty of time to change your route or find a solution. Make sure you check out the parking carefully at each location, as that will really mess up your timing if you don't allow sufficient time.

Today's top tip: map it and mark it
Unless you know the area really well, get hold of an *A to Z* map or print a road map from www.multimap.com. Mark up the routes in highlighter so you can easily refer to the map, should you need to.

Countdown Day 2
Clean-up Time

Today's task
- Clean the car inside and out.

Why do I need to do that?
- So your car looks its best on the day.

What to do
- Get into your working clothes and get to work.

What not to do
- Think it won't matter if there's a bit of mud on the back seat.

A good service

If it's necessary, you will have booked the car in to have a service either before today or today. If that's not needed, run a check of the basics – oil, water, tyres, screen wash, fuel – and top them up if necessary.

Fill up with petrol now, although if you have to do any travelling between now and the wedding you may have to top up again.

Clean it up

Start inside and give the car a thorough clean and tidy. Empty and clean out the boot, too, if you are going to have to transport anything, such as flowers or the bride and groom's luggage. Then get to work on the outside and give it a thorough wash and polish.

It's worth doing it all thoroughly today, then, if necessary, you'll only need to give it the quickest of dusting-offs on the morning of the wedding.

> **Today's top tip: assume everything will be white**
> Whether you are transporting bridesmaids or guests, they are all likely to be dressed in their best outfits, so will really appreciate the extra time you have taken to have a beautifully clean and polished car.

Countdown Day 1
The Final Countdown

Today's task
- Finish your preparations for tomorrow morning.

Why do I need to do that?
- So you are relaxed and everything goes like clockwork.

What to do
- Check the lists, collect the goods.

What not to do
- Leave it until tomorrow.

The final preparations

You've been preparing everything really carefully up to now, so don't fall at the final hurdle. All you need to do tonight is one final check through the lists to make sure you have everything ready in the right place for the morning. Visualise the day from the moment you wake up and organise everything you'll need to get you through.

You can use lists, collect items together, put Post-it Notes all over the place if you need to – anything is okay if it helps you to feel you've done everything you can. Run through the lists below and add the personal extras you feel will be useful.

The more prepared you are, the more relaxed you will feel. That way, you'll be in the best position to keep the groom relaxed and you'll both enjoy the day to the full. If anything does go wrong, you'll see it in perspective – it can't be that important since you've worked so hard to fix everything up just right. And there's always an alternative or a way round a problem.

What you need to do tonight

- If you haven't already given your gift, do it today.
- Set out your clothes ready for the morning.
- Make sure the 'ring' pocket has been unstitched.
- Set out everything else you need to take in the morning (see list opposite).
- Set the alarm for ....

- Call the groom to confirm the pick-up arrangements for the morning if you are not staying in the same place tonight.
- Check that he has all the documentation ready (licence, etc.) and money for the church fees, if necessary.
- Check that he has all his honeymoon documents and luggage ready.
- Call the ushers to check they know when to be at the ceremony venue and what their jobs are.
- Call the bride's mother or father to make sure they will bring the telemessages or any special cards.
- Charge up your mobile phone.
- Fill up the car with petrol.
- Wash the car, if necessary.
- Make sure you have arranged to collect the buttonholes and order-of-service sheets and to deliver them to the church or chief usher.
- Double-check the time you need to finish packing the car and the time you need to leave.
- The time you need to leave is ....

What you need in the morning

- Ribbons and car decorations.
- Mess-up kit and clean-up kit for the going-away car.
- The rings (placed in a designated pocket).
- Spare rings.

- Money.
- Maps.
- Mobile phone.
- Speech notes.
- Mints.
- Hip flask.
- Umbrella.
- Rescue Remedy.
- Handkerchief.
- Spare tissues.
- Camera and film.

Today's top tip: sweet dreams
Do whatever you find relaxing in the evening so you get a good night's sleep and wake refreshed and relaxed for the big day. Whether it's a hot bath, a book, a magazine or a favourite DVD, you need your beauty sleep to look and feel your best. It's best if it doesn't involve alcohol. You need to make sure the groom gets a good rest, too, so keep an eye on him and try to reassure him that everything is going to be just fine.

Countdown Day 0
The Wedding Day

Today's task
- Make sure your best friend and his bride have the time of their lives and a day to remember.

Why do I need to do that?
- Because that's your job – and because you'll have an excellent day, too.

What to do
- Remember all your plans and just stick to them. You'll be great.

What not to do
- Make any last-minute changes.

What to do in the morning

- Get up in good time.
- Have breakfast.
- If you are not with the groom, call him to make sure he is up. Confirm what time you will be over to his place to get ready, or when you will pick him up.
- Put the ribbons on the car. Fix the centre under the bonnet catch – or on the silver lady if you have a Rolls-Royce! – then tie them to the wing mirrors. Tie a bow, then leave a safe length of ribbon hanging. If it is florist's ribbon (the slightly papery sort), you can curl it (don't worry, it's really easy). If the ribbon is wide, cut it through into two or three thinner sections, then pull each piece across the blade of a pair of scissors and it will curl up.
- Put the flowers in the back of the car.
- Put the decorations for the going-away car in the boot.
- Put the clean-up kit in the boot.
- Collect the buttonholes and order-of-service sheets and deliver them to the chief usher or the ceremony venue, if necessary.
- Shower.
- Dress.
- Collect together everything you need to take (from the list above).

- Check the groom has: his going-away outfit, honeymoon documents, luggage, church fees, licences.
- Put the rings in their designated pocket.

Today's top tip: enjoy!
Everyone involved with the wedding will want it to be perfect – and nine times out of ten that's exactly what it will be. But when it comes down to it, the only important thing is that two of your best friends are making a serious commitment to each other, and sharing their vows is the only thing that has to go right to make the day special. Keep your head, and you'll encourage a calmer atmosphere, which in itself will make it more likely that things will go fine. Be the one who is reliable, reassuring, thoughtful and steady. You're going to have the most wonderful day!

Index